Exit Left

Exit Left

*Markets and Mobility
in Republican Thought*

Robert S. Taylor

UNIVERSITY PRESS

Great Clarendon Street, Oxford, OX2 6DP,
United Kingdom

Oxford University Press is a department of the University of Oxford.
It furthers the University's objective of excellence in research, scholarship,
and education by publishing worldwide. Oxford is a registered trade mark of
Oxford University Press in the UK and in certain other countries

© Robert S. Taylor 2017

The moral rights of the author have been asserted

First Edition published in 2017

All rights reserved. No part of this publication may be reproduced, stored in
a retrieval system, or transmitted, in any form or by any means, without the
prior permission in writing of Oxford University Press, or as expressly permitted
by law, by licence or under terms agreed with the appropriate reprographics
rights organization. Enquiries concerning reproduction outside the scope of the
above should be sent to the Rights Department, Oxford University Press, at the
address above

You must not circulate this work in any other form
and you must impose this same condition on any acquirer

Published in the United States of America by Oxford University Press
198 Madison Avenue, New York, NY 10016, United States of America

British Library Cataloguing in Publication Data

Data available

Library of Congress Control Number: 2016951874

ISBN 978-0-19-879873-6

Links to third party websites are provided by Oxford in good faith and
for information only. Oxford disclaims any responsibility for the materials
contained in any third party website referenced in this work.

Preface

Neo-republicanism, as two of its foremost advocates argue, is characterized by three main ideas: free persons, who are not subject to the arbitrary power of others; free states, which try to protect their citizens from such power without exercising it themselves; and vigilant citizenship, as a means to limit states to their protective role (Lovett and Pettit 2009, 12). This revivalist form of republicanism has at least two other distinctive features, though, one well remarked upon (and critically so), the other not. The first is the claim that freedom as non-domination is the defining characteristic of the classical republican tradition, the red thread that ties together its Florentine and Atlantic contributors such as Machiavelli, Milton, Harrington, Sidney, Blackstone, and some American Founders. This claim is defended by Pettit (1996, 1997) and Skinner (1998), has been thoroughly discussed, and is controversial. The second is the political character of most of their solutions to the problem of domination in human relations. What do I mean by "political" here? Roughly, the kinds of solutions classical republicans have applied to the state in order to keep it from becoming a dominating force. These political solutions have come in two forms. The first, *participatory* approach gives citizens a voice through contestatory democracy, which consists of "not only electoral rights but also the effective opportunity to contest the decisions of their representatives...[via] impartial 'courts of appeal' [that] can include the press and the streets as well as more formal channels of protest" (Lovett and Pettit 2009, 25). The second, *constitutional* approach safeguards citizens by means of the dispersal of power, such as the checks and balances associated with the separation of powers, bicameralism, federalism, and international legalism (Pettit 1997, 177–80). Neo-republicans have unsurprisingly put both of these approaches to work in the economic sphere. For example, in labor markets with concentrated employer power they have favored political solutions that are both participatory (e.g., labor involvement in managerial decisions through German-style works councils and even socialism) and constitutional (e.g., the "countervailing power" of either the state through democratic regulation or workers by means of privileges to form unions and strike) (Gourevitch 2014; Hsieh 2005; Lovett and Pettit 2009, 20–1). In sum, neo-republicans have relied heavily though not exclusively on political solutions to the problem of arbitrary power in the social, economic, and political spheres. Let us call this strategy the *political model* of republicanism.

What has been missing in the neo-republican literature is any systematic effort to explore alternative, non-political ways of limiting arbitrary power—or enough awareness of the potential risks of depending too much upon political approaches. This gap in the literature is made all the more surprising by the existence of a rich commercial-republican tradition, which has its roots in the political writings of Johan and Pieter de la Court and reaches its fullest form in those of Kant, Alexander Hamilton, and especially Adam Smith (Weststeijn 2012; MacGilvray 2011, Chapters 3 and 4). These thinkers saw commercial society in general and competitive markets in particular as means for limiting arbitrary power, ones that depended more on good institutional design than a virtuous citizenry. Unlike classical republicans such as Rousseau, who regarded the "hustle and bustle of commerce" as the prelude to slavery, Smith considered competitive markets a source of liberation from feudal dependence: the modern "tradesman or artificer," he noticed, "derives his subsistence from the employment, not of one, but of a hundred or a thousand different customers. Though in some measure obliged to them all, therefore, he is not absolutely dependent upon any one of them" (Rousseau 1997, 113; Smith 1981, 420 [III.iv.12]). Whereas Rousseau deemed the market order to be a deadly threat to republican values, Smith and other commercial republicans regarded it as an essential tool for their realization, one that required not only state support in the form of stable property rules, the enforcement of contracts, and the provision of public goods but also state refusal to micromanage the economy for the benefit of privileged rent-seeking insiders. Let us call this alternative strategy the *economic model* of republicanism.

Just as Pettit and other neo-republicans have revived and updated classical republicanism for the modern age, so this book will aspire to revive and update commercial republicanism—but in a manner that is wholly consistent with and indeed guided by a Pettit-style neo-republicanism.[1] My differences with Pettit and other neo-republicans will therefore not be over theory but instead over institutional design, especially the degree to which state protective activities work with and rely upon competitive markets. In some cases, these differences will lead to friendly amendments to the usual neo-republican policy platform, but in many others the required changes will be more substantial. As Lovett and Pettit emphasize, however, "neorepublicanism...is a research program, not a

---

[1] My choice of a cover illustration reflects these similarities and differences: just as Pettit's *Republicanism* features a Dutch Golden Age painting of Amsterdam's city hall at the time, so mine features a contemporaneous painting of a merchant shipping anchorage off the coast of Texel Island in North Holland, at some remove from Amsterdam.

comprehensive blueprint or ideology" (26), so such internal debate should not be cause for concern. Different empirical beliefs among neo-republicans, especially with regards to the form, extent, and causes of arbitrary power and the most effective remedies for it, will unsurprisingly lead to divergent policy conclusions. Such republican policy pluralism ought to be welcomed, in fact, and even if we are not eager to welcome it, it is surely inevitable in light of the "burdens of judgment" (Rawls 1993, 54–8).

Regardless, *Exit Left* will contribute further to such pluralism by building and applying an economic model of republicanism, one that is just as committed as progressive republicanism to checking arbitrary power and protecting the most vulnerable but is friendlier to the use of market mechanisms; that is, it puts more emphasis on *resourcing exit* from dominating relationships and *encouraging competition* in the spheres of family, market, and state than does the political model that is usually favored by neo-republicans. It does so by facilitating different kinds of competitive markets in each of these three domains: dating and spousal markets in the domestic sphere, labor and product markets in the economic sphere, and locational markets in the political sphere. What links these domain-specific markets together is a single, powerful idea: namely, that the effective ability to pick and choose among a variety of potential partner-providers and to exit relationships and reenter the marketplace if and when those relationships prove unsatisfactory is the best way to protect participants from arbitrary power. Extensive, empowered choice in the service of non-domination is the strategy at the heart of this economic model of republicanism. We will see this strategy unfold in diverse ways across subsequent chapters, but in each case competitive markets will act as mediating institutions ensuring that human association takes place on terms consistent with republican liberty. Far from reducing politics to economics, as some republicans might fear, this approach harnesses economics in the service of the distinctively political goal of freedom as non-domination.

Acknowledgments

First and foremost, I wish to thank Philip Pettit and Richard Dagger for their comments, criticisms, suggestions, and warm encouragement. Philip's writings on republicanism have been a constant companion over the four years I have worked on this project, and I greatly appreciated his willingness to provide feedback, whether in writing or in person, as the book developed. I am also grateful to Richard for his support and advice. Our conversations about republicanism were invaluable for determining the shape of this work, and his own writings on republicanism served as both an inspiration and a challenge. Grappling with them has made this a better book.

I also want to thank Chuck Beitz for making it possible for me to be a Visiting Fellow at Princeton's University Center for Human Values in the fall of 2013. UCHV provided a nonstop series of thought-provoking workshops, seminars, and conferences and the opportunity to discuss my project and other matters with Alan Patten, Philip Pettit, and Quentin Skinner, among others. Princeton was the ideal place to be for the early stages of this book project. I am thankful too for the office space and residential support given by Lord and Lady Sterling of Battersea during the summers of 2015 and 2016, when I finished the first and final drafts of the book, respectively.

I have been fortunate to have the opportunity to present this work to a number of different audiences, and I am grateful to them for their many insightful comments and suggestions. I have twice presented parts of this project to the Political Theory Workshop in my home department at UC-Davis, and I especially appreciated the feedback I received there from, among others, Chris Hallenbrook, Cosmo Houck, Lee McNish, Shalini Satkunanandan, John Scott, and John Warner. In November of 2013, I was invited to give an Institute for Humane Studies lecture at Clemson University on an earlier version of this project, and I want to thank Hank Clark, Brandon Turner, and Brandon Wasicsko for their remarks, hospitality, and organizational *nous* during my visit. In May 2014, I traveled to UW-Madison to do their Political Theory Workshop and Undergraduate Political Theory Association lecture, during which I received some of the best and most valuable comments on this project that I have gotten in the past four years; they helped me strengthen its central arguments and anticipate many objections. I sincerely thank Michelle Schwarze and Rick Avramenko for arranging and sponsoring my trip there, and I greatly appreciated the comments of, among others, Dan Kapust, Jimmy Klausen, Howard Schweber, and John Zumbrunnen. At APSA 2015 in San Francisco, I offered an overview of the book as part of the "Republicanism: Markets and Freedom" panel with Will Roberts, Geneviève Rousselière, and Richard Dagger as discussant; Richard's feedback was, as always, extremely helpful. Finally, in February of 2016, I did a book talk at the University of Hong Kong; my discussant, Joseph Chan, offered much sage advice, and my interactions with the audience there were very productive.

I owe a great debt to numerous others who have offered comments and recommendations, often in written form, over the last four years, including Barbara Buckinx, Simon Cotton, Frank Lovett, and two anonymous reviewers for Oxford University Press. My editor at OUP, Dominic Byatt, has made this book possible, and I thank him, Nishantini Amir, Sarah Parker, Christine Ranft, and Olivia Wells for shepherding it through the publication process. Chapter 3 contains material originally published in "Market Freedom as Antipower," *American Political Science Review*, August 2013, 107(3): 593–602, and I thank the publisher for permission to include it here. Last but certainly not least, I thank Yvonne Chiu for encouraging me to write this book—and for reminding me that books do not have to be 360 pages long. I will always be grateful for your love, support, and counsel.

Contents

Introduction	1
1. Exit, Voice, and Credibility	11
2. Family	27
3. Market	46
4. State	66
5. Republican Policy Pluralism	92
Conclusion	108
References	117
Index	127

Introduction

Arbitrary power is a pervasive feature of human societies. Women suffer in silence at the hands of domineering husbands who inflict psychological and physical abuse at will, unchecked by effective laws or cultural norms. Workers without meaningful options in life toil under the capricious rule of foremen, afraid to speak out against mistreatment for fear of losing their jobs. Residents of inner-city minority communities endure the daily humiliation of stop-and-frisks by police engaged in illicit racial profiling, while businessmen quietly pay bribes to corrupt officials with the discretion to grant or withhold essential permits. In each sphere, arbitrary power enables abuse and silences voice.

We rightly regard this subjection to others' wills with a special horror and dread, not just because it makes exploitation possible but because relationships built upon it are both mutually corrupting and morally stifling. Those people who exercise arbitrary power become arrogant and contemptuous as a consequence: they start to think of themselves as more than human, no longer bound by standards of fairness or decency, and to think of those beneath them as undeserving of respect, concern, or even simple courtesy. Those who have such power exercised over them, on the other hand, become degraded, anxious, and sycophantic: they lose their self-esteem, live with the gnawing fear of displeasing the powerful, and speak only with insincere flattery upon their lips—or with what is worse, the sincere flattery of those who have adopted their masters' views. Such mutual corruption reaches its nadir in the relationship between slaveowner and slave, but it can be found in less extreme forms in the relationships surveyed above, where it undermines the conditions necessary for reciprocity, mutual respect, and ethical development more broadly.

No contemporary school of political theory has been more focused on the singular evil of arbitrary power than republicanism, and no republican theorist has been more instrumental in the revival of this tradition of political thought than Philip Pettit, whose *Republicanism: A Theory of Freedom and Government* (1997) and *On the People's Terms: A Republican Theory and Model of Democracy* (2012) jointly present a powerful philosophical defense of distinctively republican conceptions of justice and legitimacy.[1] In these two works, Pettit defends the priority of political liberty, understood as non-domination, i.e., immunity from arbitrary power. More specifically, he argues that one agent dominates or possesses arbitrary power over another when s/he has "the capacity to interfere with impunity and at will in certain choices that the other is in a position to make" (Pettit 1996, 578). If this interfering agent's actions "track the interests and ideas of the person suffering interference," however, then such interference does *not* qualify as an exercise of arbitrary power: when I give you the key to my alcohol cupboard with explicit instructions not to return it but upon twenty-four hours' notice, you do not arbitrarily interfere with me if you refuse to return it to me immediately; rather, you act as my faithful agent, tracking my avowed interests (Pettit 1997, 55; Pettit 2012, 57). Unsurprisingly, then, the key to protecting political liberty on Pettit's understanding is to guarantee as much as possible that interferers' acts track the avowed interests of interferees, in which case those acts will be non-arbitrary.

I will discuss Pettit's theory (and certain objections to it) in greater detail later, but for the time being I want to emphasize the central role that it gives to *voice*. In Pettit's alcohol-cupboard illustration, what makes it possible for you to track my avowed interests is precisely my avowal: I provide you with explicit instructions, presumably accompanied by an explanation of why I am asking you to follow them (e.g., "I'm having trouble controlling my drinking"). Other conditions will need to hold in order for your tracking of my avowed interests to be reliable—competency conditions (e.g., skill at hiding the key) and motivational conditions (e.g., willingness to perform the role faithfully), for instance—but on Pettit's understanding of tracking the avowal condition looks to be a necessary one. Whereas arbitrary power silences voice, its negation requires voice.

His approach has immediate implications for how we evaluate state interference with our lives: such interference is arbitrary only when it fails to track "the welfare and world-view of the public" (Pettit 1997, 56). The priority of political liberty therefore requires those institutions that enable citizens to give voice to their interests and ideas, including the freedoms of speech, press, and assembly, the right to petition for redress of grievances, and most obviously the right to vote, whether for elected representatives or ballot propositions. This avowal

---

[1] I do not intend by this to downplay the important contributions of other scholars. Of special note in this regard are Quentin Skinner and Frank Lovett. Skinner's pathbreaking works (especially Skinner 1998) recover a conception of freedom as non-domination from the Florentine and Atlantic republican traditions. Lovett's writings, most recently his book *A General Theory of Domination and Justice* (2010), formalize and at times modify Pettit's theory. I will frequently engage with Lovett's work over the course of this book, as his approach is highly congenial to my own.

condition is necessary but insufficient for reliable tracking, however, because the politically powerful must also be properly motivated to respond to these expressed interests and ideas, be it through electoral competition, judicial oversight, or monitoring by pressure groups and investigatory media. As Pettit argues in *On the People's Terms*, the state will not become a dominating institution itself so long as the people share equally in control of the direction it takes, and equal control can only be secured in a properly structured constitutional democracy with a "contestatory citizenry" ready to speak out against arbitrary exercises of power (Pettit 2012, 5–6).

Is voice really the only way, however, to get interferers, be they private or public, to track the (avowed) interests of interferees? Return for a moment to Pettit's alcohol-cupboard example. Suppose that, instead of having to rely exclusively upon you as my agent, I faced a continuum of agents offering different kinds of "commitment services" at various prices and quality levels and that I could freely choose between them and *exit* from my relationships with them if they proved unsatisfactory in some way (e.g., incompetent or unmotivated). Under these circumstances, voice would be largely superfluous: my preferences would be revealed not through explicit instructions and explanations but rather implicitly, through choice and exit decisions; moreover, the pressures applied by exit would permit such a system to meet both the competency condition (wide choice and the possibility of exit would eliminate incompetent providers) and the motivational condition (exit, both actual and potential, would discipline providers). Given the right circumstances (viz., a broad array of providers with diverse characteristics and services), free choice and exit can act as effective substitutes for voice, revealed preferences as effective substitutes for stated ones, in compelling interferers to track the interests of interferees. Moreover, if exit is a live option and this is common knowledge, then it may not need to be exercised. A credible *threat* of exit may be sufficient to motivate providers, allowing exit to act not merely as a substitute for voice but as a complement to it; in other words, potential exit can empower voice, forcing providers to heed the words of their clients, be they words of instruction, explanation, or complaint.

This possible role of exit as both a substitute for voice and a complement to it can also be seen in the examples that opened this book. The surest defense against domination for women in abusive marriages is exit: so long as divorce laws are liberal, restraining orders are effective, and reasonable employment opportunities and/or alternative marital prospects are present, wives can either flee abuse or credibly threaten exit in the hope of modifying spousal behavior. Similarly, empowered workers with many job options need not tolerate abusive foremen—and if capitalists are aware of this fact, they will rein in their supervisors for fear of losing good employees. Even in cases of racist cops and corrupt officials, exit may be a real possibility, albeit one much easier for the well-heeled: because the freedom to migrate between political sub-units is a characteristic feature of open societies, especially federal ones, their exploited citizens and businesses have the option of moving from poorly-run cities, counties, and states to better-run ones; moreover, if tax revenues move with them, the administrators of these sub-units may find it in their interest to fix the problems in question, perhaps even before an exodus begins. Note that in each of these cases the right conditions must be present for exit to be effective at restraining arbitrary power: only if exit is legally enabled, economically feasible, and costly to potential abusers can it do its full job. Fortunately, however, these conditions for effective exit can frequently be created (if they do not currently exist) through a proper mix of constitutional, legal, and policy reforms; we do not need to rely on fortune, individual or social, to secure exit's benefits.

Given the promise of exit as a means of limiting arbitrary power, one might expect it to play a prominent role in contemporary republican writings, but it rarely does—and when it does, it is usually treated critically. Pettit offers numerous insightful remarks about the potential role of exit in limiting domination in the family (e.g., Pettit 2012, 158) and the market (e.g., Pettit 2007), but they are scattered and never systematized; moreover, he rejects the idea that geographic exit can limit state domination, for reasons that I will turn to in Chapter 4 (Pettit 2012, 161–2, 165–8). Lovett provides the only systematic and generally sympathetic treatment of exit in the republican literature, one that I will reference throughout the book, especially in Chapter 3 (Lovett 2010, 38–40, 49–52). Even in Lovett's works, however, exit plays a largely supporting role, and he focuses almost exclusively on its potential to curb domination in the economic sphere, with no sustained attempt to extend these insights to the domestic and political spheres.[2]

Other republicans are much more skeptical of the power of exit, whether in the economic or political spheres. Nien-hê Hsieh, for example, contends that "as an alternative to exit, workers need to be able to exercise voice—to have the capacity

---

[2] He gives notice at one point that "I will not discuss...the applications of JMD [Justice as Minimizing Domination] to questions of personal privacy, family, or gender equality" (Lovett 2010, 190). I must also mention in this context a piece by Mark Warren entitled "Voting with Your Feet: Exit-based Empowerment in Democratic Theory" (2011). Although not a republican work, Warren's article persuasively argues that the freedom to exit political parties and other civil-society organizations can reduce domination (684, 687). Like Pettit and others, Warren is highly skeptical of the ability of geographic exit (mobility) to reduce state domination (684n1, 686); given that political parties and pressure groups carry out most of their domination via the state, however, the mere ability to, say, switch parties will only go so far in limiting arbitrary power, especially where parties collude. I will return to these issues in Chapter 4.

to express dissent without exiting," which can only be accomplished if the state "provides workers with the right to contest decisions within the context of the decision-making process internal to economic enterprises," e.g., via unions; he worries that the various costs associated with exiting workplaces, including search and transition costs and the risk of unemployment and poverty, will suppress exit and thereby allow domination to persist if voice is absent (Hsieh 2005, 128–32, 134–5; cf. Dagger 2006, 162–3). Turning to the political sphere, Richard Dagger argues that the size, fragmentation, and especially high mobility associated with American cities threaten the conditions for democratic self-government and thus for the reliable tracking of citizen interests and ideas. The power of exit, rather than being a way to check arbitrary power, is instead its principal enabler: mobility detaches and alienates citizens from the places where they live and converts them into "citizen-consumers" who shop for cities as they shop for clothes, unwisely depending upon the "supposedly apolitical professionals" who run cities to offer a wide range of public services at moderate prices. Only a small, stable urban environment with public-spirited citizens can sustain republican liberty (Dagger 1997, 154–72). I will address Hsieh's and Dagger's concerns about exit in Chapters 3 and 4, respectively, but for now I should repeat what I said above: exit's effectiveness as a check on arbitrary power depends upon certain conditions, ones that might require specific constitutional, legal, and policy reforms to establish; absent these conditions, exit may fail to curb domination or even exacerbate it.

This idea that exit can be a double-edged sword, stifling voice and triggering institutional failure in some contexts but amplifying voice and sparking reform in others, is the dual thesis of Albert O. Hirschman's seminal work *Exit, Voice, and Loyalty*, the focus of my first chapter. The first part of his two-part thesis is much better known: exit may stifle voice by disproportionately encouraging the most motivated and advantaged parents, workers, voters, etc., to depart and thus abandon their more vulnerable compatriots, whose voices will be less powerful and effective as a result. His best examples of such a process are wealthier families abandoning public schools for private ones and the black middle class deserting inner cities in the wake of desegregation (1970, 45–6, 51–2, 100–2, 109–12). The second part of his thesis, however, is less well known: voice is most effective when it carries a threat (implicitly or explicitly) to impose a cost on the powerful, and exit is one of the main things that makes such threats credible, especially when it is properly resourced; potential exit can empower voice by diminishing its threshold for efficacy and thereby encouraging it (1970, 55, 82–3, 85). Return to the abused-wife example: is she not more likely to talk back to her domineering husband when exit is feasible due to liberal divorce laws, etc.? The challenge is to determine the *net* effect of exit on the security of the most vulnerable, and there is reason to believe that this relationship is fundamentally non-monotonic: it first falls with the ease of exit, as the most advantaged leave and no longer raise their voices against abuse, but then rises again as even the less advantaged are able to depart or credibly threaten to do so (cf. 1970, 83). As I will argue in this chapter, the key to protecting the most vulnerable is therefore not to thwart exit but rather to "double down" on it, providing resources to the most vulnerable that make exit easier for them (e.g., better information, travel and relocation vouchers, a basic income, etc.).

Are there other policy initiatives to help the most vulnerable that the state should pursue? Rather than empowering voice indirectly by resourcing exit, the state could try to empower voice directly by a host of means. In the economic sphere, for example, it could directly supervise and regulate labor markets, blocking certain unconscionable contractual arrangements (e.g., perilous working conditions or very long workweeks) and generally rebalancing economic power in favor of labor. Alternatively, it could strengthen labor's voice by requiring companies to have German-style works councils or other forms of labor participation in managerial decisions; less radically, it could simply encourage the formation of unions to bargain with management over wages and work conditions. I will argue against such policy initiatives in this chapter, not on the grounds of efficiency or respect for property rights but rather for the purpose of reducing domination, in this case by the state itself. As I will show, such policies necessarily give a great deal of discretionary power to (quasi-)public agents, power that can and will be frequently abused for non-public ends. With rare exceptions, the state should only empower voice indirectly, whether by resourcing exit or by encouraging competition so as to expand the range of exit options—though as I will show in Chapter 5, even these techniques can carry certain risks for republicans.

Having established the preceding theoretical framework, I will then use it over the course of the next three chapters to analyze domination and the best means for reducing it in the spheres of family, market, and state, respectively. Turning first to the family in Chapter 2, I examine the way that asymmetrical, gender-based power relations within households make women vulnerable to abuse by boyfriends and especially husbands. The principal line of defense against such abuse is the legal possibility of exit as secured by liberal divorce laws (e.g., the "no-fault" divorce laws in place throughout the USA), which have been favored by republicans from John Milton (2010) to Philip Pettit (2012, 115). But such measures are insufficient: intimidation by husbands and the risks of unemployment and poverty (especially for wives with limited job-market experience and poor marital prospects) may effectively deter exit and allow abuse to continue even where there is a formal right to leave. Whether by enforcing restraining orders, financing shelters, or offering vouchers for job (re)training, the state can take additional steps to make exit more feasible and threats of it more credible for the most vulnerable women. By contrast, *directly* enhancing voice in this context is hard to imagine. Would it require micromanagement of the household division of labor by connubial "regulators"? Legislating and then enforcing internal democracy or at least a formal proceduralism (e.g., Antioch College-style "intimacy contracts")? Even if we suspended privacy concerns, such measures would require that state enforcement agents be given a kind and degree of discretionary power that would expose couples to abuse and simply replace one kind of domination with another. If we want to minimize the sum total of private and public domination in marriage, we will need to limit the state to indirect methods of empowering women's voices.

Next, in Chapter 3, I look at the conditions for republican freedom in markets, especially labor markets. Republicans have historically been of different minds about markets: some, such as Rousseau, reviled them, while others, like Adam Smith, praised them. Present-day republicans have generally made their peace with markets, but without much enthusiasm. I will argue in this chapter that the proper republican attitude toward competitive markets is celebratory rather than acquiescent and that republicanism demands such markets for the same reason it requires the rule of law: because both are crucial institutions for protecting individuals from arbitrary interference. In the context of labor markets, where workers are vulnerable to domination from managers and capitalists, securing competition and free exit requires what I call an "Anglo-Nordic" package of policies, including informational campaigns, labor-market reform, aggressive antitrust, capitalist demogrants, and a basic income. Alternative approaches of the sort I surveyed above (e.g., labor-market regulations, works councils, and unions), which try to empower voice directly rather than indirectly, run the risk of increasing total domination by giving discretionary powers to public or private agents: these powers are required to assess where voice is being silenced and to redress it, but they can and inevitably will be misused in the pursuit of private ends, be they financial (e.g., bribery), tribal (e.g., bureaucratic-class interests), or ideological. Again, the safest approach from a republican point of view is one that resources exit and promotes competition (Taylor 2013).

I move in Chapter 4 to the third and final sphere, the state. The role of exit in minimizing state domination may seem quite limited due to its high cost, especially at the national level. This might explain why mobility (geographic exit) has played almost no role in republican defenses of federalism and political decentralization more generally, be they in the writings of Montesquieu, Rousseau, Kant, and Publius or in contemporary works.³ However, the cost of exit is much lower from political sub-units such as cities, counties, and states/provinces, and the freedom to migrate between them is a characteristic feature of open societies, especially federal ones; such relatively low exit costs and free movement even describe some international systems such as the EU, apart from language barriers. In such contexts, exit can offer a means of escape from state domination for both citizens and businesses, as I argued earlier. Also, if political institutions are designed so that exit imposes heavy costs on the leaders of those political sub-units—if they lose tax revenue as a result, say, whether directly or via revenue-sharing systems—then the voices of citizens and businesses will be indirectly empowered, and leaders will find it in their interest to be responsive and pro-active about abuse. Some of the policy initiatives discussed above, especially travel and relocation vouchers, can do double or even triple duty across the three spheres, in fact, providing resources for exit whether the source of abuse is domestic, economic, or political. To be sure, the role of voice remains extremely important in the political sphere and increasingly so as we move from local to state to national governments: at this point in time, at least, escaping from abusive national governments is quite hard for all but major corporations and a global elite; as a result of this, exit exerts little discipline on nation-states, aside from narrow policy arenas (e.g., corporate taxation). Still, I will argue in this chapter that, with good institutional design and resourced exit, market-like mechanisms can play a larger role than normally thought possible in disciplining the state and restraining arbitrary power, a role that becomes increasingly important the lower we go in the hierarchy of political sub-units and the more those sub-units resemble firms competing for mobile "citizen-consumers" in a locational marketplace (cf. Dagger 1997, 154).

Even if policy instruments are well chosen, however, and focused on indirectly enhancing voice through expanded choice and resourced exit, state domination remains an ever-present risk, especially as the state grows in size and power. First, even the policies I recommended above are liable to abuse because their execution requires discretionary power: when we examine antitrust authorities or welfare administrators, we will see their need for discretion in selecting targets for prosecution or in determining eligibility for benefits, discretion that can be

---

³ Contemporary republicans are eerily silent on the issue of federalism. It receives favorable mention by Pettit (1997, 179) and a few others, but with little explanation other than a repetition of traditional republican concerns about the centralization of power as a threat to liberty. I should note that, in contrast to the political-theory literature, mobility plays a key role in the economic literature on federalism: see, for example, the important works of Buchanan (1996), Weingast (1995), and especially Tiebout (1956), which I will discuss in Chapter 4.

directed towards non-public ends. Second, even if these problems can be avoided (by rendering benefits unconditional, for example), the state will still have to raise revenues to fund the policies, and the more revenue it needs to raise, the more difficult raising it will be due to tax avoidance and evasion, which will itself require increasing the power and discretion of revenue agents. Lastly, the more powerful a state becomes—the more it can command persons and resources via taxation and regulation—the more attractive a target it ends up being for capture by rent-seeking interest groups, who can then turn its public power to non-public purposes. Greater state power, even for initially benign ends, can enable greater domination and subsequent abuse of unorganized interests by organized ones.

Once republicans recognize these public-choice insights, they will see the need to adopt a comparative-institutional method. If escalating state efforts to counter private power with public power will at some point increase rather than decrease total domination, then republicans will be forced to weigh the evils of private domination against the evils of the public kind at the relevant legislative and policy margins. Rawlsian "burdens of judgment" will inevitably come into play at this point: even when republicans are assessing the same evidence, they will disagree with each other about the required tradeoffs (Rawls 1993, 54–8). Among the causes of disagreement will be their differing assessments of the nature and extent of private domination, of the efficacy of state responses to such domination, and of the possibility of keeping the state and its agents limited by genuinely public purposes as state power grows. In short, even if republicans share the very same normative and theoretical commitments, they will arrive at rather different conclusions about the proper size and scope of state power: some will be small-government republicans, like Friedrich Hayek (1960), while others will be big-government ones, like Michael Sandel (1996, 2012). This reasonable pluralism in republican policy commitments will be the subject of Chapter 5.

These considerations suggest a modest approach to international republicanism, to which I will briefly turn in the Conclusion. Republicans of all stripes should be able to coalesce around a minimal global republicanism dedicated to free trade and free migration as means for checking arbitrary power, be it economic or political, at the national level. Economic concentration and the opportunities it creates for dominating consumers and employees are less problematic when trade and migration are free, as global competitors in product, service, and labor markets will find it in their own interest to limit the market power of would-be national monopolists and monopsonists. Free migration also offers a refuge to the victims of totalitarian and authoritarian regimes around the world, which remain the greatest threats to republican liberty internationally.

Granted, this is a stopgap measure, but one that, in combination with political criticism and economic pressure, can eventually encourage the internal political changes that will finally allow these nations to be integrated into the global order of open societies. Ever mindful of Kant's warning that a world state would be a "soulless despotism" and a "graveyard of freedom" (1996, 336 [8:367]), we can instead focus our political energies on the less ambitious but also safer project of fostering global competition and the free movement of products, people, and ideas across borders, whose success would be a humble but worthwhile approximation of Kant's own inspiring republican vision.

1

Exit, Voice, and Credibility

Albert Hirschman's *Exit, Voice, and Loyalty* (1970) was his single most influential book, though its impact was much greater in political science and sociology than in his home discipline of economics (Adelman 2013, 446–9). Over the decades, it has received even more citations than his landmark study in development economics, *The Strategy of Economic Development* (Hirschman 1958).[1] Whereas the latter work questioned existing orthodoxies in that field, including its practitioners' moves toward more rigorous mathematical modeling, the former took broader aim at the parent discipline. In it, Hirschman condemns "the economist's bias in favor of exit and against voice" and singles out Milton Friedman's educational-voucher scheme for special attention (Hirschman 1970, 16–17). Friedman, Hirschman complains, sees "withdrawal or exit [from underperforming schools] as the 'direct' way of expressing one's unfavorable views of an organization. A person less well trained in economics might naively suggest that the direct way of expressing views is to express them!" Relatedly, he also takes Friedman to task for denigrating democratic alternatives to exit (which Friedman dismisses as "cumbrous political channels" [1962, 91]), asking "what else is the political ... process than the digging, the use, and hopefully the slow improvement of these very channels?"

So far, so familiar to Hirschman's readers. What may be less well remembered is that he levels even stronger criticism at political theorists and practitioners for their own peculiar sins:

But the economist is by no means alone in having a blind spot, a "trained incapacity" (as Veblen called it) for perceiving the usefulness of one of our two mechanisms. In fact, in the political realm exit has fared much worse than has voice in the realm of economics. Rather than as merely ineffective or "cumbrous," exit has often been branded as *criminal*, for it has been labeled desertion, defection, and treason.   (Hirschman 1970, 17; cf. 98, 109–12)

---

[1] The former had 18,020 citations and the latter 9,990 as of June 2016 (http://scholar.google.com/); they together make up over half of Hirschman's Google Scholar citations. *The Rhetoric of Reaction: Perversity, Futility, Jeopardy* (1991), which I will discuss at the end of this chapter, comes in a distant sixth at 1,330 citations.

For this reason, he announces that one goal of his book is to "demonstrate to political scientists the usefulness of economic concepts" like exit (19).

In this chapter and throughout the remainder of my book, I hope to revive this neglected aspect of Hirschman's project by demonstrating to republican political philosophers the utility of exit as a mechanism for limiting domination in the domestic, economic, and political spheres. I will begin by reviewing the dual theses of *Exit, Voice, and Loyalty:* the first, better-known thesis that "the presence of the exit alternative can tend to atrophy the development of the art of voice" as well as the second, lesser-known thesis that "if voice is to be at its most effective, the threat of exit must be credible, particularly when it most counts" (43, 85). I'll then go on to argue that the *net* effect of exit on the security of the most vulnerable members of society, even if it is initially negative, can be made positive by cutting exit's cost to such a point that even the vulnerable can take advantage of it or at least credibly threaten to do so. Finally, I will warn against the adoption of policies that, rather than empowering voice *indirectly* by cutting exit's cost, try to empower it *directly* by a number of means. As I will maintain, such policies necessarily give a great deal of discretionary power to (quasi-)public agents, power that can and frequently will be abused in the pursuit of non-public ends. If the state wishes to minimize overall domination (both private and public), it should limit itself to empowering voice indirectly by resourcing exit and encouraging competition so as to expand the available range of exit options for the vulnerable. Working with rather than against the grain of competitive markets will prove to be the best means of advancing progressive republican ideals.

Hirschman's Dual Theses

Hirschman's first thesis is the best known and the one most frequently associated with the book, especially by its many fans in political science and sociology. As he declares in his pithiest rendering of it, "the actual level of voice feeds on *in*elastic demand, or on the lack of opportunity for exit" (34). Hirschman's central concern here is that *exit will undermine voice* across a variety of social contexts by encouraging the most motivated and advantaged participants to depart when institutions start to fail, in the process abandoning their most vulnerable associates, whose voices will be less powerful and effective as a result.[2] Whether we

---

[2] Republicans are generally partial to a *prioritarian* interpretation of freedom as non-domination: that is, they recognize the importance of providing greater protection for the more vulnerable members of society (for example, Lovett 2010, 201; Pettit 2012, 89–90). For the purposes of this book, I will also adopt this prioritarian reading. For a broader defense of prioritarianism, see Parfit 1997.

consider the customers of a bungling state-monopoly railroad or the stockholders of an underperforming corporation, the lesson is the same: "those customers who care most about the quality of the product and who, therefore, are those who would be most active, reliable, and creative agents of voice are for that very reason also those who are apparently likely to exit first in case of deterioration" (44–7; cf. 55).

Hirschman's most powerful—and disturbing—examples of this phenomenon at work all involve deepening divisions of class and race. Consider first his education example: specifically, parents choosing between public and private schools for their children. If public schools begin to deteriorate for whatever reason:

> increasing numbers of quality-education-conscious parents will send their children to private schools. This "exit" may occasion some impulse toward an improvement of the public schools; but here again this impulse is far less significant than the loss to the public schools of those member-customers who would be most motivated and determined to put up a fight against the deterioration if they did not have the alternative of the private schools. (45–6)

Given the expense of private education, these parents will likely be wealthier than average, too, thereby increasing the existing income stratification between public and private schools (45n2). Moreover, exit (or the threat of exit) will be a much more effective disciplining device in private education than in public, further exacerbating quality differences between the two: "exit is not a particularly powerful recuperation mechanism in the case of public schools—it is far more so in that of private schools which have to make ends meet" (52). Thus, deterioration in public schools when private schools are an exit option can trigger a runaway process, one characterized by ever-escalating quality and income stratification caused by the most motivated and advantaged parents abandoning the public sector.

Next consider his neighborhood-decline example, which involves a toxic combination of class and racial division. Hirschman begins with an overall description of the problem:

> When general conditions in a neighborhood deteriorate, those who value most highly neighborhood qualities such as safety, cleanliness, good schools, and so forth will be the first to move out; they will search for housing in somewhat more expensive neighborhoods or in the suburbs and will be lost to the citizens' groups and community action programs that would attempt to stem and reverse the tide of deterioration. (51)

Beginning in the 1960s, racial desegregation in the United States—residential, occupational, and educational—started to provide educated middle- and upper-class black families a path out of the ghetto, but as certain members of the Black Power movement noticed at the time, these improved opportunities for talented individuals levied costs on the group: by removing their best educated, most civically-active residents, integration helped place black-majority districts on a downward-spiraling trajectory of neglect, decline, and further "black flight" (109–12).[3] In this case, at least, the promise of escape from racial apartheid was both a blessing and a curse, though for different segments of the black population.[4]

These two examples and others Hirschman uses in his book diminish exit's appeal, but as I hope to show, what he takes away with one thesis he basically gives back with the other. Given how little noticed this second thesis has been, I shall start with Hirschman's rendering:

> The chances for voice to function effectively as a recuperation mechanism are appreciably strengthened if voice is backed up by the *threat of exit*, whether it is made openly or whether the possibility of exit is merely well understood to be an element in the situation by all concerned.... [While] the *effectiveness* of the voice mechanism is strengthened by the possibility of exit... the threat of exit must be credible, particularly when it most counts. (82–3, 85)

In other words, voice is most effective when it (implicitly or explicitly) carries a threat to impose a cost on the underperforming institution, one that will be noticed by its managers, and exit is the key thing that makes such threats credible, especially when it is properly resourced and therefore practicable. To put it differently, exit can *empower* voice by lowering its threshold for efficacy and thereby encouraging it. Consider divorce, for example: if a husband knows that his wife can feasibly exit the marriage (due to "no fault" divorce laws, shelters, restraining orders, good work and/or marital opportunities, and so on), he is much more likely to listen to her complaints and modify his behavior—but if so, that makes her voice more effective and consequently more likely to be put to use.[5] Thus, in cases such as this one, exit might very well be "off the equilibrium

---

[3] This "black flight" was paralleled by "white flight" from the inner cities. Although racism played the principal role in the latter, even a "moderate urge to avoid small-minority status" could have triggered it (Schelling 1978, 154).

[4] A very closely related phenomenon can be found in the precipitous decline of HBCUs (Historically Black Colleges and Universities), whether in terms of student enrollment, endowments, surviving institutions, or even SAT scores. As Charlayne Hunter-Gault (2014) explains, HBCUs "once held a monopoly. Today, they struggle to compete with elite colleges that have stepped up recruiting for the best and brightest black students."

[5] See Weinstock (2001, 81) for an application of this lesson to political secession: geographically-based minorities are more likely to have their complaints about majority abuse heeded when they enjoy an entrenched right to secede.

path," to use the language of game theory: if the threat of exit is credible and the abusive parties therefore yield, the threat won't have to be exercised, that is, no exit will occur.[6] As Hirschman himself notes, the threat may not even have to be explicitly made: even if "the possibility of exit is merely well understood to be an element in the situation by all concerned," offenders may *preemptively* yield in order to avoid the risk of potential exit (82). Thus, when exit is effectively resourced and this fact is common knowledge, silence can sometimes speak as loudly as words.

With Hirschman's second thesis in view, we can now see that exit's *net* effect on voice is likely to be ambiguous in sign: exit may remove the best and most driven backers of institutional change, depressing the overall exercise of voice (first thesis), but it can also render the voices of those who remain behind more effective, thereby encouraging their exercise (second thesis). For our purposes here, however, we should be focusing on a slightly different desideratum: not voice per se, but rather *the security of those most vulnerable to institutional failure*. How is *this* likely to vary with the cost of exit? As I'll suggest here and argue throughout the book, the relationship will be a non-monotonic one: that is, the security of the most vulnerable will initially suffer when the cost of exit falls from a prohibitive level because the most advantaged will then leave and no longer raise their voices against abuse, but it will rise again if the cost continues to fall to a point that permits even the least advantaged (and therefore most vulnerable) to exit or at least credibly threaten to do so. In short, a falling cost of exit will first decrease and later increase the security of the most vulnerable, holding out the possibility that at a low enough cost of exit their security may actually be greater than it was when exit was prohibitively expensive and all individuals, the most and least advantaged alike, were trapped together in dysfunctional institutions.

As the earlier divorce example suggests, however, exit costs are not brute facts of nature, outside our control; rather, their level is partly determined by public policy, and legal and policy reforms can therefore potentially lower them. For an abused wife, the right to unilaterally initiate divorce proceedings—and the knowledge that the exercise of this right will be insulated through state provision of various protective services (shelters, restraining orders)—will unambiguously lower the cost of exit and thereby empower voice. Were the right merely a formal one, we might wonder whether it would not redound to the benefit of abusive

---

[6] Whether exit will be off the equilibrium path or not will depend upon many factors, including whether information (for example, about the value of available actions to affected parties) is symmetric, parties are rational, and so on.

husbands, who could threaten to leave dependent wives in penury at a moment's notice, but so long as exit costs are *sufficiently* reduced through protective services, "community property" rules that guarantee wives an equal share of jointly acquired assets, state provision of welfare benefits and job retraining, and so on, even a vulnerable wife can exit or credibly threaten to do so and be better off than she would have been in a world where divorce was illegal. What this suggests is that the solution to the problem of the suppression of vulnerable voices by exit (first thesis) may be *more* and *better resourced* exit, not less, because if the cost of exit can be reduced enough, vulnerable voices will be empowered in a manner that leaves them better off than they would have been in an exit-free world. Hirschman's second thesis, in short, has the potential to give exit back the good reputation that his first thesis took away.

In light of this finding, let us now revisit Hirschman's education example and Friedman's voucher proposal. If the most motivated and advantaged parents abandon failing public schools, it is indeed likely that the least advantaged will suffer—but why? On Hirschman's reading, this occurs for two interrelated reasons: first, the least advantaged lack the financial means to follow the most advantaged out of the failing state schools and must therefore remain behind with their diminished voices; second, state schools are much less responsive to exit pressures than private schools are, so that the threatened departure of advantaged parents will do little to improve them, further widening the income and quality gaps between the private and public sectors. As I noted above, however, these are not brute facts of nature; rather, they are the result of deliberate policy choices. Suppose instead that the least advantaged *did* have the financial means to join the most advantaged and that public schools *were* reasonably responsive to exit pressures. How might this be brought about? Any policy reform that allowed parents to exit underperforming state schools with their per-capita share of educational expenditures for that school (or, better, with an income-scaled share so that poor parents received much more than rich ones) would have this tendency: it would give poor parents the means to escape bad public schools, and it would make those bad schools pay the price in terms of reduced resources; this latter effect could even be heightened by tying administrator and teacher salaries to their available resources, putting every educational tub on its own bottom, as with private schooling. Friedman's voucher proposal would be one way to achieve this, but other, less radical approaches are also available, including public-school-choice systems that use charter and magnet schools in combination with free parental choice of schools to pluralize public provision and encourage competition and accountability. Here, lowering exit costs and enhancing responsiveness can place otherwise vulnerable parents and their children in an even better position than they would occupy in a world that denied exit to both rich and poor.[7]

What if this last claim is incorrect, though? That is, what if the just-described alternative world of universal "free exit" was actually *worse* than a "no-exit" world? Perhaps a world where rich and poor are trapped together in public schools is better for the poor than free exit because in a free-exit world income and quality stratification will still exist (albeit in a more tempered form than in a "partial-exit" system of escape for the wealthy alone), but in a no-exit system everyone would be in the same boat and would consequently be properly motivated to row together for the common good. Even if this idealized picture of a no-exit world were accurate, we would have to ask whether it was politically feasible, and in this case (and others to be discussed throughout the book), it is highly unlikely to be so. First, the right to send one's children to private schools has been constitutionally entrenched for nearly a century (see *Pierce v. Society of Sisters* [1925]), so the children of the rich cannot be dragooned into the public-school system against their parents' will. Second, even if they could be coercively enrolled in public schools, their parents would still have the option of self-segregation by income *within* the state system given (1) the very localized nature of educational finance, at least in the USA, where per-pupil expenditures vary enormously across school districts, and (2) free residential mobility across those same districts, which is also constitutionally entrenched (see *Saenz v. Roe* [1999]). Even in the unlikely case that educational finance became significantly more centralized, there would still be a great deal of exit (whether to the private sector or within the public sector via residential mobility) by the well-heeled. Thus, the choice is not between free-exit and no-exit worlds; rather, it is between free-exit and partial-exit worlds—between a world where everyone has the ability to exit and a world where only the advantaged have that ability—and the former is clearly preferable if we prioritize the protection of our most vulnerable citizens against institutional failure.

We started this section by examining the legitimate concerns of both Hirschman and his many devotees in political science and sociology about the tendency of exit to silence vulnerable voices (first thesis). As we have seen, however, exit can also empower those voices by rendering them more effective (second thesis), and policy reforms that reduce the cost of exit for the most

---

[7] The most respected analysis to date of charter-school performance, produced by Stanford's Center for Research on Education Outcomes (CREDO 2013), finds that charter-school students who are in poverty and/or English-language learners enjoy "significantly stronger growth in reading and math than their counterparts in TPS [traditional public schools]" (76–7). Similar results have been found in randomized controlled trials: see, for example, Gleason et al. (2010, 9–12).

vulnerable and improve the responsiveness of institutions via competition can make their threats of exit increasingly credible and thus persuasive, whether in the context of abusive marriages or deteriorating public schools. This potential role of properly-resourced exit in improving security for the most vulnerable against neglect and abuse at the hands of violent spouses, cosseted state employees, and others in positions of power should be of special interest to republican political theorists, who seek to minimize domination by making interference by authority figures track the avowed interests of those with whom they interfere. As Hirschman's second thesis demonstrates, exit can act as a complement to voice, giving vulnerable citizens a persuasive means to sway and even check the exercise of arbitrary power.... and failing this, it can provide a substitute for voice, offering a means of escape from such power, if only it is properly resourced.

Defining and Differentiating Exit and Voice

Before discussing direct versus indirect strategies for empowering voice, I would like to pause for a moment and turn to something that has been done only implicitly so far: defining and differentiating exit and voice. I delayed this task until now because our everyday understandings of exit and voice were sufficient to make Hirschman's examples intelligible. From this point on, however, we need to be a little more precise in how we define them, distinguish them from each other, and differentiate their subtypes so as to avoid confusion. Here are Hirschman's definitions:

Management [of a dysfunctional organization] finds out about its failings via two alternative routes:

(1) ... some members leave the organization: this is the *exit option*. As a result, revenues drop, membership declines, and management is impelled to search for ways and means to correct whatever faults have led to exit.

(2) ... the organization's members express their dissatisfaction directly to management or to some other authority to which management is subordinate or through general protest addressed to anyone who cares to listen: this is the *voice option*. As a result, management once again engages in a search for the causes and possible cures of members' dissatisfaction. (1970, 4)

Exit, then, is separation: the attempt not simply to leave a dysfunctional organization but also to escape its authority and the various obligations of membership in it. Voice, on the other hand, is standing one's ground, staying and fighting for change within an organization, which can take a variety of forms: speech (for example, criticisms, reform proposals), organization (for example, rallies, caucuses), voting (such as elections, recalls), and the like. As we saw previously, all of these have their analogues in the spheres of family, market, and state.

Moreover, in each of these spheres, exit and voice can take both legal and illegal forms. Consider the political sphere, for example. (I will look at the economic sphere [labor markets] in the next section.) Legal forms of exit include emigration from a nation-state or internal migration across political jurisdictions in a federal system; giving up membership in a political party might also qualify. Legal forms of voice will include petitions, protests, running for office, and voting. Some illegal forms of exit might be described as "exiting in place," be they complete or partial, violent or non-violent: a citizen might (partially) exit the state (or one of its jurisdictions) *without moving*. Secession would generally be a complete, violent form of "exiting in place," as might a rebellion or revolution; at the other extreme, civil disobedience would be a partial and non-violent form: the peaceful, public, and conscientious refusal to obey certain laws because they (or maybe other laws) are unjust. Pettit, despite his generally skeptical attitude toward exit in the political sphere (2012, 161–2, 165–8), believes that these illegal forms of exit can serve as a check on the abuse of state power: "to the extent that the possibility of popular, successful resistance is on the cards—to the extent even that it is on the cards as a matter of common belief—the influence of the people over government can be established on a robust basis and can constitute a real form of power" (2012, 173; cf. 137–40, 174, 202, 219–20, 223, 225).[8] Illegal varieties of voice are also common in the political realm, ranging from the overstepping of reasonable bounds on rights of speech, press, and association (for example, unfurling an anti-capitalist banner from a corporate building during an Occupy protest) to the corruption of officials (by means of bribery, blackmail, and so on).

It can be difficult at times to distinguish between exit and voice, especially in the political sphere. For example, if a voter decides not to vote, or perhaps even refuses to register, is that exit or voice? One could think of it as a sort of "exiting in place," because the voter decides to remain in a jurisdiction but reject the responsibilities of active citizenship. Silence can often be a potent way of voicing one's opinion, however, not unlike a deliberately spoiled ballot, say, or a vote for "none of the above." This ambiguity may explain why some scholars treat voting inconsistently. Mark Warren, for example, classifies the "right to vote" as a "voice-based inclusion" at one point in a recent article (2011, 683), but then deems "voting for a nonincumbent party or candidate" to be a "form of exit" ten pages later (693). For simplicity, I will always regard voting as a kind of voice in this book, but I do recognize that in certain contexts or given certain motives it

---

[8] Strictly speaking, Pettit does not consider civil disobedience to be a form of "resistance," but instead a limit case of "contestation, a way of opposing laws within the system" (2012, 137–8).

might be better treated as a type of exit. Similar things might be said of other political actions, for example, revolt: is it violent, peremptory voice or an attempt to escape from existing authority without moving? I will have more to say about these myriad kinds of exit and voice, how they relate to one another, and their ambiguities over the course of the book, but they are sufficiently delineated for now.

Direct versus Indirect Empowerment of Voice

I said earlier that voice is most effective when it (implicitly or explicitly) carries a threat to impose a cost on an underperforming institution, one that will be noticed by its managers, and that exit is the *key* thing that makes such threats credible, especially when it is properly resourced and therefore practicable. Are there not other means, though, of making threats credible? As the previous section indicated, there are many illegal ways to empower voice through increasing the credibility of threats, such as a history of violence when demands are not met, but set these aside for the time being. In many societies, voice is directly empowered by the institutions of electoral democracy: competitive elections, universal suffrage, freedoms of speech, press, and assembly, public financing of campaigns, and the like. These institutions give citizens a means to influence the state without exiting: if state agents do not heed the public's voice, they may be removed from office by angry voters, whether directly (elected representatives) or indirectly (political appointees). If this direct form of empowerment works in the political sphere, why not extend it to the economic sphere, say, by various reform measures? More generally, why can't the *direct* empowerment of voice supplement, substitute for, or even entirely replace the *indirect* empowerment exit offers?

The answer, in brief, is that such empowerment threatens even greater domination, not by private agents, but rather by public (or quasi-public) agents. As Pettit warns, "while the state has to guard people against private domination... it also needs to guard against itself practicing a form of public domination" (2012, 3). He identifies "three dangers" that may lead to such domination:

The first is the danger of elected politicians usurping the influence of the people under motives of self-interest. The second is the danger of private lobbies usurping that influence out of a desire to push government in a direction that does not necessarily have popular support. And the third is the danger that unelected authorities... might gain a hold over government policy that is not sensitive to popular demands. (2012, 231–8, here 231)

The first two dangers will be familiar to students of public-choice economics: legislators, in their pursuit of winning electoral coalitions and/or bribes, will do the bidding of factions instead of the general public, commonly by passing inefficient laws that have concentrated benefits but diffuse costs, such as protective tariffs, agricultural subsidies, and tax breaks (2012, 232–5; cf. Buchanan and Tullock 1962, 283–95). In such cases, the state itself is effectively captured and used by rent seekers as an instrument of domination and exploitation.

Even if legislators were saintly, however, the third danger would offer yet another point of access for private interests of many sorts due to the *discretionary power* necessarily possessed and exercised by unelected authorities. As Pettit reminds us:

> The fact that in practice many decisions will have to be left to government under the best imaginable regime of popular control raises the spectre of abuse in this range of discretion. Abuse might consist in the authorities smuggling some self-serving candidates into the set of policies between which a decision has to be made in any area, or indeed keeping some popularly acceptable candidates out of that set. Or it might involve the authorities taking advantage of loopholes in the process available to resolve policy disputes in any area for their own special benefit or the benefit of cronies. (2012, 176; cf. Lovett and Pettit 2009, 23–4)

Even public-spirited legislation will need to be implemented by unelected authorities—be they political appointees or bureaucrats with civil-service protections—and that implementation will necessarily involve discretionary power: the implementing authorities will have to interpret laws, pick enabling policies, and decide how (and even whether) to enforce those policies in particular contexts, given limited implementation and enforcement resources (see Hamburger 2014). Also, no amount of guidance and oversight by elected executives, legislatures, and courts can possibly ensure that this power will always be used for its intended ends given the immense ambition and complexity of modern legislation. Unelected officials will therefore often be able to abuse their sizable discretion in pursuit of non-public ends, whether financial (for example, bribes or offers of future employment from those they regulate), tribal (such as the protection of bureaucratic-class interests by, for example, a mutual agreement to slow down work in order to boost leisure and cut stress), ideological (for example, the alleged harassment of so-called "patriot" groups by the Internal Revenue Service [IRS]), and so on.

I want to emphasize here that it is their *ability* to abuse, not actual abuse, that constitutes domination. As Pettit affirms, "the grievance I have in mind is that of having to live at the mercy of another, having to live in a manner that leaves you vulnerable to some ill that the other is in a position arbitrarily to impose" (1997, 4–5). Such vulnerability is wholly consistent with that other rarely or never engaging in such abuse; even authoritarian political systems sometimes have civil services that are rather clean (for example, Singapore). The problem is that so long as civil servants (such as police officers and tax officials) have the kind of discretionary powers described above, those who are subject to their authority are quite likely to fail what Pettit refers to as the "eyeball test," that is, the ability to "look others in the eye without reason for the fear or deference that a power of interference might inspire" (2012, 84; for example, see Dewan 2014 on IRS use of civil-forfeiture laws).

But how are these dangers related to the direct empowerment of voice? Consider a labor-market example. Suppose we were to discover that workers in a particular industry (such as hospital nurses) were subject to the monopsonistic or oligopsonistic power of local employers and were therefore vulnerable to domination and exploitation. One way of rectifying this would be indirect empowerment of their voices by enhancing their exit options through travel/relocation vouchers, antitrust laws, capitalist demogrants, a basic income, and so on. Direct empowerment of voice would be another possibility, though, whether as a supplement to or a substitute for indirect empowerment. It might take the form of state supervision and regulation of workplaces in order to prevent abuse (call this the "regulation option") or of mandatory labor participation in decision-making, up to and including labor representation on corporate boards (call this the "participation option").

Let us first look at the regulation option, which attempts to rebalance the power of capital versus labor with the police powers of a democratic state. In uncompetitive labor markets of this kind, capitalists and their managerial agents will be in a position to exercise arbitrary power over their employees. A democratic state may, through detailed workplace rules, counter such power, but given that this conflicts with the interests of capitalists and managers, workplaces will have to be carefully monitored to ensure compliance, and regulatory agents will need powers to match in order to both *assess* (via surprise inspections and video surveillance, say) and *redress* (by jail time, fines, or perhaps just new or modified rules) the employer abuse that silences labor's voice. But such powers run the risk of increasing overall (that is, private plus public) domination, because monopsonistic and oligopsonistic firms are now exposed to the same sort of arbitrary power that they exercise over their own employees: regulatory agents, given their wide remit to stop abuse, must be granted discretionary powers of a kind that can themselves be readily abused, especially in light of the complexity of the regulatory task and the limited ability of other state authorities to provide effective oversight due to that complexity. Regulators might use these powers to demand bribes from employers in return for leniency, to pursue the interests of their bureaucratic class in future employment in the industry as consultants, or even to harass employers as part of personal or ideological vendettas. Unsurprisingly, republicans are well aware of these risks. Frank Lovett, for example, maintains that these "workplace regulations" and other efforts to "regulate...social relationships," while perhaps useful for stopping certain "gross abuses," will often just substitute one form of domination for another:

> There will always be discovered new and ever-more subtle means of converting material advantage into domination. In the long run it is unlikely that public policy could ever keep pace with, much less anticipate, such innovations—except perhaps with a regulatory structure so dense and intrusive as to raise serious objections on other grounds. (For starters, a state powerful enough to accomplish this task might itself become a great source of domination.)   (Lovett 2009, 825–6)

In contrast to intrusive workplace monitoring and intervention, government delivery of resources that empower workers in labor-market choices can remain largely aloof from relations within the firm, trusting instead that free exit will discipline owners and managers and prevent them from dominating their employees.

Turning now to the participation option, we can see the same logic at work, leading to the same dangers. The democratic state can demand that monopsonistic or oligopsonistic employers include employees in their decision-making processes (such as via German-style "works councils"), but because such inclusion is contrary to their business interests, the state will once again have to give regulators the necessary discretionary powers to monitor, assess, and redress employer non-compliance. Else, employers will just create procedural "workarounds" to bypass the influence of laborers: managers are ultimately responsible to the owners who hire, fire, and promote them, and thus in the absence of effective state monitoring and enforcement they will follow their lead, not that of labor.[9] As we have seen, though, these same monitoring and enforcement powers can be abused by regulators, threatening an increase in overall domination. Again, state provision of resources that empower workers (for example, capitalist demogrants that allow them to set up their own businesses, perhaps along participatory lines, or at least credibly threaten to do so) offers a safer way to protect them from the market power of monopsonists and oligopsonists.

---

[9] This problem might be solved if workers *were* the owner, as in associational market socialism. But the transition to socialism can itself create enormous risks of state domination, especially given the likely resistance of capitalists and landowners to property confiscation: either the state must become powerful enough to expropriate the expropriators, threatening everyone's liberties, or it will be recaptured by these ruling classes in a similarly dangerous reactionary backlash. (The 1973 Allende/Pinochet "transition" in Chile provides an instructive historical example of the latter.)

Direct empowerment might take a third form, however, one in which the state encourages (or perhaps just ceases to oppose) the creation of countervailing forms of market power; call this the "privatization option." In a labor market with a monopsonist, for example, the state might try to encourage the formation of a union monopolist to counter its market power. It could do this by no longer applying antitrust laws to unions, by enforcing closed-shop and union-shop agreements (which would otherwise be conspiracies in restraint of trade), by requiring employers to engage in collective bargaining with their organized employees, or even by turning a blind eye to union violence or threats of same. The resulting bilateral monopoly would restrain discretion but leave wage determination to the relative bargaining power of the two sides (Nicholson 1995, 729–30). Such an arrangement would have the advantage of removing state regulators with easy-to-abuse discretionary powers from the scene, but only if rights to organize were protected across *all* labor markets: if workers needed a state discovery of monopsony or oligopsony power in their industry in order to unionize, then we would once again need state regulators with discretionary powers of monitoring, assessment, permitting, and enforcement to make such a determination and grant the required permissions—but as we saw with the regulation and participation options, these powers are readily abused in the service of non-public ends.

Therein lies the rub, however. The danger of directly empowering voice is not necessarily decreased by replacing state power with non-state (here, union) power: fighting fire with fire still risks burning all involved. This fact is apparently why Pettit dislikes what he calls the "reciprocal power" strategy for minimizing domination, which involves countering private power with more private power (1997, 67–8). Pettit's understandable concern with this kind of solution is that by it "arbitrary interference and domination may be reduced, but it is not ever going to be eliminated," because the residual mutual interference involved fails to "track the interests and ideas of those who are affected" (67). Even worse, systematic government efforts to enhance the market power of one side against the other may have the (net) effect of increasing domination, especially given that, as I just noted above, the only way to avoid reintroducing state regulators with discretionary powers is to allow workers to unionize across all labor markets, including those where employers lack significant market power and where unionization would therefore *increase* the capacity for domination and exploitation, in this case of employers by employees.

The case I've just made against the regulation, participation, and privatization options is preliminary and admittedly sketchy, so I will have more to say about them in Chapter 3; I'll also look at analogous options in the domestic and political spheres in Chapters 2 and 4, respectively. At this point, however, I should indicate that if these three options were the only alternatives to doing nothing *and* if we believed that the market power of employers was a much more serious problem (actually and potentially) than that of employees, then we might be justified in pursuing one or more of them with caution in the hope that the *net* effect would be to reduce the scope for domination and exploitation. But as I've argued so far in this book and will continue to argue in the chapters ahead, these are not our only options, which is fortunate given the serious risks they involve. The indirect empowerment of voice by promoting competition and resourcing exit is an attractive alternative, one that involves substantially less risk of exacerbating the very problem it seeks to solve—though certainly not zero risk, a caveat to which I will return in Chapter 5.

The Rhetoric of Reaction?

Given that this chapter began by trumpeting its concern for the most vulnerable, readers may be forgiven for wondering whether the policy preferences expressed throughout—including support for school choice and skepticism regarding labor-market regulations, co-determination, and even unions—are really consistent with such concern, especially in light of their association with political forces that often appear more interested in the welfare of the most advantaged than that of the most vulnerable. Even worse, I have helped myself (especially in the previous section) to a form of argument that Hirschman has labeled "the single most popular and effective weapon in the annals of reactionary rhetoric," viz. the *perversity thesis*: "any purposive action to improve some feature of the political, social, or economic order only serves to exacerbate the condition one wishes to remedy" (1991, 7, 140). Do these features of my book's text hint at a darker, more reactionary subtext?

As for my employment of the perversity thesis, we should recall what Hirschman himself repeatedly said about it:

To show how advocates of reactionary causes are caught by compelling reflexes and lumber predictably through set motions and maneuvers does not in itself refute the arguments, of course.... The fact that an argument is used repeatedly is no proof, to be sure, that it is wrong in any particular instance. I have said so here and there already, but it bears repeating quite bluntly and generally: there certainly have existed situations where well-intentioned "purposive social action" has had perverse effects.... (1991, 164, 166)

I believe that existing institutions and current proposals for the direct empowerment of voice are in precisely these "situations": as I have argued and will continue to argue, direct empowerment runs the risk of increasing net domination—and even barring this possibility, it is less effective at reducing it than indirect empowerment because it subdues private domination only at the cost of inadvertently enabling a certain amount of the (quasi-)public kind.

Moreover, by making the case for indirect empowerment, I am making a case *for* reform, not against it. Nor is indirect empowerment a recipe for laissez-faire; rather, it demands specific forms of state action across a range of social contexts—domestic, economic, and political. What is true is that these reforms will require a redirection of state interventions so that they work with rather than against the grain of competitive markets, and to this degree they may overlap with the policy preferences of some on the political right. This overlap doesn't make the policies any less progressive, but it does make them more pragmatic, and appropriately so: progressives should be open to adopting whatever policies appear likely to improve the security of the most vulnerable, even if they rely more heavily on market forces than progressive policies heretofore have. Much as John Roemer thinks that "socialists have made a fetish out of public ownership" and that "the choice of property rights over firms and other resources is an entirely instrumental matter, which should be evaluated by socialists according to their various propensities to induce the [equalities] with which socialists are concerned" (1996, 307), I fear that progressives have made a fetish out of social democracy and have as a result given insufficient attention to other means of reducing domination and exploitation. This book is intended as a corrective, then, to this tendency, for the benefit of progressives generally and progressive republicans more specifically. The market may ultimately prove to be a better friend to the most vulnerable than the forum, as counterintuitive as this possibility will undoubtedly be for progressives of all stripes (cf. Elster 1986).

2

Family

The family has long been used as a model for the state in Western political thought, from Plato's *Republic* (Plato 1991, 140-3 [461d-463e]) to Filmer's *Patriarcha* (Filmer 1991)—but it has long been seen as an anti-model as well. As John Stuart Mill acidly remarked in *The Subjection of Women*, "the family is a school of despotism":

> The law of servitude in marriage is a monstrous contradiction to all the principles of the modern world, and to all the experience through which those principles have been slowly and painfully worked out. It is the sole case, now that negro slavery has been abolished, in which a human being in the plenitude of every faculty is delivered up to the tender mercies of another human being, in the hope forsooth that this other will use the power solely for the good of the person subjected to it. Marriage is the only actual bondage known to our law. There remain no legal slaves, except the mistress of every house. (1991, 518, 557-8)

This depiction of marriage may seem exaggerated to us, but it is a perfectly accurate description of the status of married women throughout most of Western history, including Mill's nineteenth-century England, and in much of the world today. The Roman *paterfamilias* model, in which the male head of household had absolute power over the persons and possessions of all other family members, be they wives, children, or servants—including the power of life and death—has been a persistent influence on family law in the West; though its most extreme features were gradually curbed by legal reform and custom, the powers of the male head of household were still immense until relatively recently (Frier and McGinn 2004). Even in Mill's England, "all [women's] rights, all property, as well as all freedom of action" were transferred to the husband upon marriage; the husband was deemed as legally responsible for his wife's actions as "for the acts of his slaves or of his cattle" and was therefore permitted the use of physical coercion to discipline his wife or to return her to his household were she to flee; marital rape was not punishable; wives had no legal rights over their children; and legal separation, much less divorce, was very difficult to obtain for the rich and essentially impossible for others (Mill 1991, 503-6).

The legal status of women, married or unmarried, has obviously improved tremendously in the last century and a half, especially in the West. Nowhere is this more evident than in trends in divorce laws. Divorces were rather rare in Western society before the late nineteenth century, apart from a brief period of legal liberalization during the French Revolution (Phillips 1988, xiii). Marital exit for women in abusive (or simply loveless) relationships ranged from very difficult to impossible depending upon time, place, and economic class. The twentieth century saw a slowly accelerating liberalization in divorce laws, however, culminating in the move to no-fault divorce in most Western societies during the 1960s and 1970s (Phillips 1988, 561–72). Women are now no longer legally trapped in violent marriages, and their protections *within* such marriages have also substantially improved. As a result, domination of wives by husbands has been sharply curtailed.

Curtailed, but hardly eliminated. First, violence against female partners in the USA is still high: although such violence (excluding homicides) declined by 71 percent between 1994 and 2011, there were still 4.7 victimizations (involving simple assault, aggravated assault, robbery, or rape) per 1000 females age twelve or older in 2011 (Catalano 2013, 1). This violence, as well as the threat of it, remain an important mechanism of control over married women. Second and relatedly, the so-called "covenant-marriage" movement has tried, with only limited success so far, to undercut the universal availability of no-fault divorce and thereby increase the exit costs and diminish the bargaining power of women in abusive relationships (Nock et al. 2008). Finally, even where no-fault divorce endures, the marital-exit right is often merely formal: intimidation by husbands and the risks of unemployment and poverty (especially for wives with limited job-market experience and poor prospects for remarriage) may effectively discourage exit and allow abuse to continue, even where there is a legal right to leave—and the presence of dependent children can make this already difficult decision still more so.

Against these ongoing opportunities for domestic domination, the republican tradition has long provided and continues to provide the intellectual resources for resistance. John Milton, for example, offered one of the earliest defenses of a form of no-fault divorce on the simple ground of incompatibility ("unfitness... and contrariety of mind") and in doing so linked marital freedom to the political kind:

> He who marries, intends as little to conspire his own ruin as he that swears allegiance: and as a whole people is in proportion to an ill government, so is one man to an ill marriage. If they, against any authority, covenant, or statute, may by the sovereign edict of charity save not only their lives but honest liberties from unworthy bondage, as well may he against any

private covenant, which he never entered to his mischief, redeem himself from unsupportable disturbances to honest peace and just contentment. (Milton 2010, 99, 370)

As Milton's language indicates, however, his main concern was the marital freedom of men who were, like himself, trapped in an "ill marriage" (Phillips 1988, 119–26). Two centuries later, his countryman John Stuart Mill turned his attention to the plight of women within these marriages; his *Subjection* delivered a scathing critique of marital despotism that is republican in spirit if not in letter (Lovett 2010, 45, 54, 138; Pettit 1997, 139). Mill decries the legal servitude of wives, who suffer under a masculine power more minute, extreme, and degrading than that traditionally exercised by slaveowners. He acknowledges that the best husbands, like the best slaveowners or dictators, will be led by sympathy and affection to refrain from exercising their absolute power in an abusive fashion (like Torvald in Ibsen's *A Doll's House*—see Pettit 2014, xiii–xv), but he also hastens to remind us that:

laws and institutions require to be adapted, not to good men, but to bad.... It would be tiresome to repeat the commonplaces about the unfitness of men in general for power, which, after the political discussions of centuries, every one knows by heart, were it not that hardly any one thinks of applying these maxims to the case in which above all others they are applicable, that of power, not placed in the hands of a man here and there, but offered to every adult male, down to the basest and most ferocious. (Mill 1991, 507, 509)

The vulnerability of women to such arbitrary marital power, and the need to curtail it in order to promote freedom as non-domination within households, continue to motivate republican thinkers to this day (e.g., Lovett 2010, 51, 54 and Pettit 2012, 115, 158), but unfortunately this has not led them to engage in any systematic theorizing about it.[1] In the present chapter, I will try to fill this gap in the contemporary republican literature.

I begin by reviewing the details of Pettit's conception of freedom as non-domination or antipower, focusing on both his understanding of power and the institutions he regards as crucial bulwarks against it (Pettit 1996). I then turn in the succeeding section to marital power versus marital freedom, i.e., those conditions that facilitate domestic domination and exploitation versus those that hinder them and, in the limit, even negate them. As we shall see, marital freedom will require not only formal rights of marital exit but also methodical efforts to enhance competition in dating and marriage markets, open labor

---

[1] Lovett in fact explicitly says that "I will not discuss...the applications of JMD [Justice as Minimizing Domination] to questions of personal privacy, family, or gender equality" (Lovett 2010, 190). Also, some partial exceptions to my claim of a "gap" in the literature here would include Costa (2013, 923, 926, 929, 931–2), Laborde (2008, 165–6), and Phillips (2000, 288–90).

markets to women by underwriting job retraining and fighting employment discrimination, and resource exit by means of shelters, travel and relocation vouchers, a basic income, etc. In the penultimate section, I argue that marital freedom is itself a kind of antipower on Pettit's own understanding of the term and then respond to two objections: first, that *direct* empowerment of women's voices within households is to be preferred to indirect empowerment via enhanced competition and resourced exit; second, that focusing on marital exit threatens to further erode marriage and exacerbate social atomization. Finally, in the conclusion I briefly look at the limits of the exit model for both wives and household dependents (e.g., minor children and the elderly).

Freedom as Antipower

In his seminal essay "Freedom as Antipower," Pettit contends that "one agent *dominates* another if and only if he or she has a certain *power* over that other: in particular the power to interfere in the affairs of the other and to inflict a certain damage" (Pettit 1996, 578 [emphasis added]). More specifically, an agent has **power** over another whenever three jointly-sufficient conditions are met, viz., when an agent has:

1. "the capacity to interfere
2. with impunity and at will
3. in certain choices that the other is in a position to make" (Pettit 1996, 578, 581).

Liability to the exercise of such power is what republicans mean by the term "vulnerability."[2]

Let us review these three conditions in order. Pettit takes the "interference" in "capacity to interfere" to be "a more or less intentional attempt to worsen an agent's situation of choice" by means of, for example, coercion or manipulation, where "context fixes the baseline by reference to which we decide if the effect is indeed a worsening" (Pettit 1996, 578–9). To interfere in this sense "with impunity" is to do so without "penalty," be it resistance by the victim, punishment by

---

[2] See, for example, Pettit's use of this term (1997, 5, 122–5, 145). Vulnerability in this technical sense should not be confused with vulnerability more generally. For instance, the fact that certain coastal residents might be vulnerable to hurricanes does not necessarily imply that they are vulnerable in the republican sense—unless the first kind of vulnerability creates the second (e.g., their distress after a hurricane makes them vulnerable to monopolistic pricing). Relatedly, I will maintain in Chapter 3 that the fact that workers may be vulnerable to firing without cause does not necessarily imply that they are vulnerable in the republican sense—unless they work within non-competitive labor markets produced by employer collusion, the absence of affordable exit options, etc.

some external authority, etc. (Pettit 1996, 580). To interfere "at will" is to do so "at [one's] own pleasure... [or] whim"; in other words, the interferer has the necessary "discretion" to act as he or she chooses (Pettit 1996, 580, 587). Such a capacity to interfere with impunity and at will, when "fully realized," "amounts to an absolutely arbitrary power" (Pettit 1996, 580). Finally, this capacity for arbitrary interference will "vary in extent as well as in intensity," i.e., it will differ by domain (e.g., household, economy, government) and by degree (Pettit 1996, 581). Pettit refers to all of this as the "*procedural* sense" of power (Pettit 1997, 55). This procedural sense is later supplemented by a *substantive* one, viz., that what (also) characterizes arbitrary interference is a failure to "track the interests and ideas of the person suffering interference"; therefore, Ulysses' sailors are not interfering arbitrarily with him when they tie him to the mast, because by doing so they "track [his] interests and ideas."[3]

In order to secure freedom as non-domination, we must seek *immunity* from such power, i.e., **antipower**, by means of three related strategies. First, "we may compensate for imbalances by giving the powerless protection against the resources of the powerful" (Pettit 1996, 589). The most important institution for doing so will be a "nonvoluntaristic rule of law," in which laws must meet criteria of "generality, transparency, nonretroactivity, and coherence," so that no individual or group can use the law manipulatively as a means to dominate others (Pettit 1996, 590). Second, we might counter power "by regulating the use that the powerful make of their resources," whether in the spheres of family, market (e.g., policy measures "against monopoly power"), or state (e.g., "limitation of tenure, rotation of office, separation of powers") (Pettit 1996, 589–91). Last, we may compensate "by giving the powerless new, empowering resources of their own," including particular "welfare-state initiatives" (e.g., "universal education... social security, medical care, accident insurance") (Pettit 1996, 591–2). He concludes by observing that these three categories of measures can and often do take informal, non-state forms, including the pressures applied by various social, economic, and political movements "and even competitive market forces" (Pettit 1996, 592). Although he mentions competitive markets merely in passing here, I will argue in this chapter as well as the next two that encouraging effective competition in marriage markets, labor markets, and even locational markets can counter the dominating effects of marital, market, and political power, respectively.

---

[3] Pettit 1997, 55; cf. 184. Pettit describes this elsewhere as a failure to "track the interests I am disposed to avow" (Pettit 2006b, 135–6). Analogously, he states that arbitrary interference *by the state* fails to track "the welfare and world-view of the public" (Pettit 1997, 56).

Marital Power versus Marital Freedom

As I noted in the introduction, the power of husbands over wives was enormous for much of Western history, coming shockingly close to Pettit's "absolutely arbitrary power" (1996, 580). Consider, for example, domestic violence. Roderick Phillips, in his magisterial history of divorce in Western society, points out that the Roman law "had originally given the husband the right to kill his wife if she committed certain offenses, notably adultery"; in fact, as late as 1907, French law "permitted a husband to kill his wife with impunity if he did so on discovering her in the act of adultery" (1988, 324). In general, however, by the early-modern period:

> a husband no longer had the right to kill his wife, but his position as her superior did endow him with the right, indeed the duty, to chastise or punish her using physical means. In part this right was justified in terms of the legal obligations borne by the husband to answer for his wife's actions; because he was thus personally responsible for her misdeeds, it was considered reasonable that he should have the right to control her behavior and to repress her when necessary.... The notion of "moderate correction" developed, permitting a husband to beat or otherwise physically chastise his wife "moderately," as distinct from excessively. Lethal weapons were ruled out, and a rule developed to the effect that if a stick or rod were used, that it should be no thicker than a man's thumb. (This is the origin of the term "rule of thumb.")   (Phillips 1988, 324–5)

Not until the nineteenth century did Western nations begin to forbid such "moderate correction," and even at that time Mill remarked that "the vilest malefactor has some wretched woman tied to him, against whom he can commit any atrocity except killing her, and, if tolerably cautious, can do that without much danger of the legal penalty" (Phillips 1988, 330–44; Mill 1991, 508). Given this legal liability to moderate correction, in which wives could be corporally punished by their husbands at will within loosely enforced limits, wives' legal liabilities in many other areas—for example, regarding property, children, and so forth—are hardly surprising. They were effectively treated as minors by the law until the twentieth century, in the custody of their husband-masters and consequently subject to their every whim.

Given these aspects of the sexual contract, we may wonder why women entered and then stayed in such relationships. At least in part, the answer was a lack of options, be they economic or legal. First, women were exposed to formal and informal labor-market discrimination, which severely limited their employment options and ensured continuing dependence on their fathers or husbands; discrimination was usually even more extreme for married women, who were assumed to have duties within their households that were inconsistent with employment (Lovett 2010, 54). For instance, labor-force participation for all US women in 1890 was only 18 percent, and for married women it was a paltry 5 percent; for comparison, the female labor-force participation rate in Jordan is now 15 percent, one of the lowest in the world (Phillips 1988, 615; World Bank 2014). Thus, the only real alternative to a poor, childless spinsterhood with heavy if not complete financial dependence on the father was marital despotism, entered with hope that the husband's arbitrary power would be gently exercised (Pateman 1988). Second and relatedly, only in the late nineteenth century did rudimentary welfare states begin to emerge in the West, and not until well into the twentieth did women in most Western countries have welfare support as a potential alternative to dependence on fathers and husbands; of course, such dependence on the welfare state created its own risks of domination and exploitation (Brown 1995; Noble 1997). Third, as discussed earlier, divorce was very difficult or even impossible to obtain for most of Western history; only in the past century has no-fault divorce become the Western norm, giving women at least the legal means of escape from abusive (or simply loveless) marriages (Phillips 1988, xiii, 561–72). Fourth, even if divorce had been obtainable, divorced wives would until fairly recently have had no rights to alimony, community property, or even their own children, so divorce would have meant the abandonment of both their financial security and their progeny (Phillips 1988, 628). Last but not least, for most of Western history women have been socialized to think that marriage and motherhood are their highest callings in life, making exit from a specific sexual contract or from the sexual contract in general a harrowing choice (Mill 1991, 493–501; Pateman 1988).

The contemporary Western world is obviously a very different place now for women, be they married or unmarried. A revolution has occurred in the realms of occupation and education: in the United States, for example, women are now the majority in managerial, professional, and related occupations, and they receive approximately half of all law and medical degrees and the majority of university degrees in general, from associate to doctoral degrees; there has even been a convergence in earnings, and most of the gap that remains is better explained by the structural features of certain kinds of jobs (viz., inflexible hours and non-linearity of earnings with respect to time worked) than crude employment discrimination (Goldin 2014). Welfare states have been founded and expanded, divorce laws have been fully liberalized, and the aftermath of divorce has been made much fairer in terms of support payments, property division, and child custody. Even women's socialization has undergone dramatic change thanks to feminism, with career becoming co-equal with marriage and motherhood (Goldin 2006). All of these changes have put women in a much better position to postpone marriage, to reshape its internal culture, and to exit it when it no longer serves their needs.

In the wake of all this progress, however, there is a risk of complacency. As I noted in the introduction, partner violence against women remains a problem, despite dramatic improvements in the past two decades. Additionally, residual labor-market discrimination and the still-gendered household division of labor (e.g., on a typical day in 2013, only 19 percent of US men did housework, compared to 49 percent of women [Bureau of Labor Statistics 2014, 2]) suggest that at both work and home, men collectively retain certain historical privileges and powers. Such inequalities continue to put women at a disadvantage in entering, negotiating, and exiting marriages, and to the extent this is true, wives are still vulnerable to domination and exploitation by their husbands. Marital power remains a pressing social problem, in short, and we must seek solutions to it if we hope to advance marital freedom.

The principal means of defense against such domination and exploitation is still marital exit. As Pettit, abridging Milton, tells us, "marriage could be free only if divorce was possible: that is, only if there was a possibility of release from the marriage bond—and from subjection to the rights and powers of a spouse—in the event of estrangement between the two parties" (Pettit 2012, 158). Recall Hirschman's second thesis: voice is most effective when it carries a threat (be it implicit or explicit) to impose a cost, and exit is the key thing that makes such threats credible, especially when it is properly resourced and therefore feasible. In other words, exit can empower voice by lowering its threshold for efficacy and thereby encouraging it. If a husband knows that his wife can exit the marriage, he is much more likely to listen to her complaints and modify his behavior—but if so, that makes her voice more effective and consequently more likely to be put to use. The shift to no-fault divorce throughout the West during the 1960s and 1970s amplified women's voices by giving them a right to end their marriages unilaterally by simply leaving their husbands and living separately for a minimum specified period; they were no longer required to prove marital misconduct, such as adultery or cruelty, to receive a divorce (Phillips 1988, 560–5). This abandonment of moralistic divorce policies and the simultaneous transfer of divorce powers from church and state to spouses themselves helped to liberate married women, who now had the ability to either exit unhappy marriages or credibly threaten to do so, thereby strengthening their voices within marriage as well as promoting overdue changes in marital culture.

These revolutionary changes to divorce laws were accompanied by a dramatic increase in the US divorce rate, which rose from 2.2 divorces per 1000 population in 1960 to a peak of 5.2 in 1980, then fell back to 3.4 in 2009; a bit fewer than half

2

Family

The family has long been used as a model for the state in Western political thought, from Plato's *Republic* (Plato 1991, 140–3 [461d–463e]) to Filmer's *Patriarcha* (Filmer 1991)—but it has long been seen as an anti-model as well. As John Stuart Mill acidly remarked in *The Subjection of Women*, "the family is a school of despotism":

> The law of servitude in marriage is a monstrous contradiction to all the principles of the modern world, and to all the experience through which those principles have been slowly and painfully worked out. It is the sole case, now that negro slavery has been abolished, in which a human being in the plenitude of every faculty is delivered up to the tender mercies of another human being, in the hope forsooth that this other will use the power solely for the good of the person subjected to it. Marriage is the only actual bondage known to our law. There remain no legal slaves, except the mistress of every house. (1991, 518, 557–8)

This depiction of marriage may seem exaggerated to us, but it is a perfectly accurate description of the status of married women throughout most of Western history, including Mill's nineteenth-century England, and in much of the world today. The Roman *paterfamilias* model, in which the male head of household had absolute power over the persons and possessions of all other family members, be they wives, children, or servants—including the power of life and death—has been a persistent influence on family law in the West; though its most extreme features were gradually curbed by legal reform and custom, the powers of the male head of household were still immense until relatively recently (Frier and McGinn 2004). Even in Mill's England, "all [women's] rights, all property, as well as all freedom of action" were transferred to the husband upon marriage; the husband was deemed as legally responsible for his wife's actions as "for the acts of his slaves or of his cattle" and was therefore permitted the use of physical coercion to discipline his wife or to return her to his household were she to flee; marital rape was not punishable; wives had no legal rights over their children; and legal separation, much less divorce, was very difficult to obtain for the rich and essentially impossible for others (Mill 1991, 503–6).

The legal status of women, married or unmarried, has obviously improved tremendously in the last century and a half, especially in the West. Nowhere is this more evident than in trends in divorce laws. Divorces were rather rare in Western society before the late nineteenth century, apart from a brief period of legal liberalization during the French Revolution (Phillips 1988, xiii). Marital exit for women in abusive (or simply loveless) relationships ranged from very difficult to impossible depending upon time, place, and economic class. The twentieth century saw a slowly accelerating liberalization in divorce laws, however, culminating in the move to no-fault divorce in most Western societies during the 1960s and 1970s (Phillips 1988, 561–72). Women are now no longer legally trapped in violent marriages, and their protections *within* such marriages have also substantially improved. As a result, domination of wives by husbands has been sharply curtailed.

Curtailed, but hardly eliminated. First, violence against female partners in the USA is still high: although such violence (excluding homicides) declined by 71 percent between 1994 and 2011, there were still 4.7 victimizations (involving simple assault, aggravated assault, robbery, or rape) per 1000 females age twelve or older in 2011 (Catalano 2013, 1). This violence, as well as the threat of it, remain an important mechanism of control over married women. Second and relatedly, the so-called "covenant-marriage" movement has tried, with only limited success so far, to undercut the universal availability of no-fault divorce and thereby increase the exit costs and diminish the bargaining power of women in abusive relationships (Nock et al. 2008). Finally, even where no-fault divorce endures, the marital-exit right is often merely formal: intimidation by husbands and the risks of unemployment and poverty (especially for wives with limited job-market experience and poor prospects for remarriage) may effectively discourage exit and allow abuse to continue, even where there is a legal right to leave—and the presence of dependent children can make this already difficult decision still more so.

Against these ongoing opportunities for domestic domination, the republican tradition has long provided and continues to provide the intellectual resources for resistance. John Milton, for example, offered one of the earliest defenses of a form of no-fault divorce on the simple ground of incompatibility ("unfitness... and contrariety of mind") and in doing so linked marital freedom to the political kind:

He who marries, intends as little to conspire his own ruin as he that swears allegiance: and as a whole people is in proportion to an ill government, so is one man to an ill marriage. If they, against any authority, covenant, or statute, may by the sovereign edict of charity save not only their lives but honest liberties from unworthy bondage, as well may he against any of all marriages now end in divorce in the USA (Amato 2010, 651). The reasons for this increase remain in dispute, though there is an emerging consensus that no-fault divorce was a cause, but not a major one, and that its effect has faded with time (Allen and Gallagher 2007, 1). Despite this, a worrying backlash against no-fault divorce has occurred among numerous evangelicals, Catholics, and even feminists. For example, when New York became the last American state to adopt no-fault divorce in 2010, the opposition to it included not just the Catholic Church but the state chapter of the National Organization for Women (Pappas 2010). I will address the concerns of feminists and religious conservatives about no-fault divorce later in the chapter, but for the time being I want to focus on a policy innovation at the state level that has been strongly supported by religious conservatives: covenant marriage. Covenant-marriage legislation was adopted by Louisiana in 1997, Arizona in 1998, and Arkansas in 2001, though its progress has since stalled. Covenant marriages are a return to an older model of marriage and divorce, but they now exist side-by-side with contemporary models of marriage that retain no-fault divorce. In Louisiana, for example, couples may choose a covenant marriage characterized by premarital and marital counseling requirements as well as a higher threshold for obtaining a divorce, viz., either fault (e.g., adultery, abandonment, and physical or sexual abuse) or a two-year separation (as opposed to the six-month separation required in a standard marriage) (Nock et al. 2008). The worry here is that, by increasing exit costs, covenant marriage will silence women's voices, especially in already unequal relationships. Early studies of these marriages are not encouraging on this score: covenant marriages are more likely to be characterized by gender dominance and subordination than standard marriages, for example, although this may largely be the result of self-selection by gender traditionalists into covenant marriage (Baker et al. 2009). If we are interested in preserving marital freedom, our first task should be to avoid policy changes such as this one, which runs the risk of making already vulnerable women even more so.[4]

Even if no-fault divorce is, as I have argued, the most important means to counter marital power, it is far from being a sufficient means, and it might in some situations *increase* women's vulnerability, which may explain some of the feminist opposition to it. If the right to marital exit is merely formal and can be unilaterally exercised by either spouse, then it may redound at times to the benefit

---

[4] Even policy changes that may seem only tangentially related to power relations within marriage, such as restricting access to birth control and abortion, are likely to disadvantage wives: if such restrictions make it more probable that they will have unplanned pregnancies, then given the burdens of pregnancy and early motherhood and the associated vulnerabilities both physical and psychic, they are likely to become more dependent upon their husbands as a result.

of abusive husbands, who could threaten to leave their dependent wives in penury at a moment's notice, thereby gaining enormous bargaining power within their marriages. There is some evidence, in fact, that stay-at-home mothers were especially disadvantaged by the shift to no-fault divorce (Grossbard-Shechtman 1995, 94–5; cf. Pappas 2010). The problem we face here is the same one described in Chapter 1: non-monotonicity in the relationship between exit costs and the welfare of the least advantaged. The welfare of dependent wives might at first decrease, and only later increase, as exit costs fall; that is, the move from an effectively no-exit world to a partial-exit one may hurt dependent wives, even if a further move to a free-exit world would help them. The solution is also the same as Chapter 1's: shifting from a merely formal right of marital exit to a substantive one, which would empower the voices even of dependent wives.[5] In order to accomplish this, we must not only *promote competition* in both labor and dating/marital markets but also *resource marital exit* by means of various government services and income transfers.

Consider first how stoking competition in various kinds of markets would lower marital exit costs. As we discussed earlier on, gender discrimination in labor markets can trap women in abusive marriages. Great progress has been made on this front, but there is much left to do. For example, recent structural changes in some professionals' work (e.g., pharmacists, veterinarians, pediatricians) towards increasing flexibility and greater linearity of earnings with respect to time worked have disproportionately benefited women and helped close the wage gap. These changes have been driven in part by economies of scale and pressures to reduce labor costs, but they have also occurred due to employee pressure (Goldin 2014, 1116–18). This evolution of the workplace could be catalyzed by steering government contracts to firms with more flexible work schedules, for example. Doing so would further diminish the wage gap and therefore improve the prospects of currently dependent wives who are considering marital exit.

Enhancing competition in dating and marital markets themselves may be as important, if not more so, than enhancing it in labor markets, especially for dependent wives with little work experience. Consider the case of women within insular ethnic and religious minorities who have been socialized from an early age to marry within their communities, who face internal marriage "markets"

---

[5] Rawls argues in a similar vein that in order to preserve the worth of the basic liberties (and defend them against the charge of "radical democrats and socialists" that they are "merely formal"), we must extend adequate material means for their exercise to all, including especially the least advantaged (1993, 324–31).

that are rigged against them, and who may be subject to emotional and even physical coercion when choosing marriage partners. As Susan Okin has claimed, multiculturalism may be bad for women, especially if it means insulating such groups from liberal-rights enforcement and public education (Okin 1999). On the other hand, efforts to open up such internal marital markets may fall afoul of important associational rights guaranteed to all citizens, rights that may help to protect minority groups and their members from other forms of domination (e.g., domination by the majority or by other, more powerful minorities). Fortunately, there are available policies that not only respect such equal associational rights but also safeguard "minorities within minorities" (Eisenberg and Spinner-Halev 2005). For example, reasonable requirements for civic education during childhood can inform these women of their rights and make them aware of the existence of, and the opportunities in, the larger society (Rawls 1993, 199–200); additionally, the kinds of government services and income transfers discussed below can limit coercion and offer means of escape. The challenges that insularity and gender traditionalism pose for such dependent women have decreased over time thanks to better education and law enforcement and to the tools made available by the Internet (including dating sites such as Match.com and eHarmony, which can be secretly and therefore safely accessed), but more can be done to provide these women a broader array of options, marital and otherwise.

In addition to advancing market competition, states can resource exit by delivering both essential services and income transfers. First, given the ongoing problem of partner violence, it is essential that the government protect women from physical coercion, whether through the use of restraining orders and police protection or by financing women's shelters; without these services, exit may be too dangerous for them (Pettit 2012, 115). Second, in the aftermath of divorce, states must ensure a fair division of property and future income by enforcing alimony and child-support payments and by instituting "community-property" rules (including, perhaps, the 50/50 division required by California law); both would help protect the financial interests of stay-at-home wives who by forgoing employment limit their labor-market options and put themselves at a bargaining disadvantage vis-à-vis their working spouses (Phillips 1988, 628; cf. Pappas 2010). Third, states could offer vouchers specifically designed to enhance exit options, whether indirectly (e.g., ones for job retraining or vocational education more generally) or directly (e.g., ones for travel and/or relocation, which will have the side benefit of sustaining market and political freedoms, too—see Chapters 3 and 4). Finally, states could guarantee conditional or unconditional basic incomes to allow dependent women with minimal job-market experience to support themselves, at least for a while, without working (Lovett 2010, 199–203;

Pettit 2007). All of these measures, both resource and competition related, can operate together to make marital exit a feasible option for dependent wives. Without them, the liberating potential of no-fault divorce will remain underdeveloped for the most vulnerable class of married women.

Marital Freedom as Antipower

As I have indicated from time to time in this chapter, state efforts to promote competition and resource exit are essential for creating vibrant marriage markets, i.e., markets for spouses. If the state recognizes a formal right of marital exit but does nothing to liberalize labor and dating markets or assist vulnerable women with support services and income transfers, then dependent wives will be excluded from the usual benefits of competitive markets: here, the effective ability to pick and choose among a variety of potential partners and to exit relationships and reenter the spousal marketplace if and when those relationships prove unsatisfactory. Such marital freedom contrasts with the marital power that characterized the rigged, monopsonistic marital markets of the past, where masculine collusion—abetted by church and state—placed women at a dangerous disadvantage, limiting their options and enabling their subordination and exploitation. Tragically, such cartel-like behavior continues today both in traditional societies and in certain insular ethnic and religious minorities within liberal immigrant nations, and as the drive for covenant marriage makes clear, there are some religious conservatives who would like to reestablish patriarchy, this time masked by the pretense of marital pluralism.

Although I will have more to say in Chapter 3 about the domination-curtailing effects of competitive markets in general, for the time being I want to emphasize the ways that competitive marital markets in particular have this effect. In fact, such markets are antipower in Pettit's exact sense: specifically, their participants have no ability to interfere at will and with impunity in the choices of the other participants (Pettit 1996, 578, 581). They have no ability to interfere at will because the ready availability of attractive alternatives (e.g., other spouses, or independent living underwritten by gainful employment) narrowly confines this interference: once-dependent wives now have many options, permitting them to credibly threaten exit; husbands, aware of this fact, must show restraint and consideration—and if they fail to do so, they will bear the costs of their wives' exit, which is proof that they can no longer interfere with impunity. These characteristics of competitive marriage markets make them antipower not just in Pettit's procedural sense but in his substantive sense as well: such markets maximize "not the gain from marriage compared to remaining single for any particular marriage, but the average gain across all marriages," thereby "tracking the interests" of market participants in one important way (Becker 1973, 824–5). This efficiency property of marriage markets hinges, of course, on a host of conditions (including full information, the absence of collusion, etc.), which explains why a republican state that prioritizes the interests of its most vulnerable citizens must work diligently to maintain them (Becker 1993).

Given the challenge of preserving these conditions, though, we may wonder whether the indirect empowerment of women's voices through enhanced competition and resourced exit will be sufficient to prevent domination. For example, despite the advances of the last several decades in women's capacity to exit abusive marriages, domestic violence continues to be a serious social problem, prompting feminists and other activists to criticize the police for being too reluctant to intervene in domestic disputes. The 1994 Violence Against Women Act was enacted in response to such concerns; among other things, it encouraged states to adopt mandatory arrest policies that allow cases against domestic abusers to move forward in the courts even without the cooperation of victims (Cho and Wilke 2005). These policies are an example of what I called the "regulation option" in Chapter 1: direct empowerment of women's voices by means of state supervision and regulation of households, in this case triggered by complaints of domestic violence. The efficacy of the VAWA has been questioned by some, however (e.g., Koss 2000), and the 71 percent decline in intimate partner violence between 1994 and 2011 may simply track the overall decline in violent crime over the same period—or even be the result of increasingly credible threats of marital exit, which may have stayed the hands of potential abusers (Catalano 2013, 1). Still, few would deny any role whatsoever to direct empowerment. Even Frank Lovett, who is highly skeptical of state regulation of social relationships as a solution to domination, acknowledges that it may well be appropriate in cases of "gross abuse" like this one (Lovett 2009, 825–6). The more vital question, however, is whether it can serve as a *general* solution to the problem of marital domination, i.e., one that can mostly or even entirely replace indirect empowerment via enhanced competition and resourced exit, and here there is reason for doubt.

Consider first the regulation route for direct empowerment of women's voices within the household. Through direct supervision and regulation, the state could try to counter the power of domineering husbands; one might imagine "marital regulators" carrying out this task, somewhat akin to the social workers employed by child protective services to perform household visits and check on the welfare of mistreated minors. Though such an approach might raise few objections as a temporary response to documented cases of domestic violence, as a more general solution to household domination it will likely prompt concerns about both privacy and paternalism. Family privacy is an essential condition for creating intimacy and trust within the family and cultivating a rich internal culture, be it religious or secular (Peterman and Jones 2003); it is hard to imagine reconciling such privacy with the pervasive presence of marital regulators. As for paternalism, genuinely voluntary forms of domination among consenting adults, whether S&M or religiously motivated (but reflectively endorsed) gender traditionalism, ought to remain beyond the purview of state regulation, however uncomfortable they may make us. Again, it is tough to conceive how marital regulators would be able to show enough discernment to reliably distinguish between the voluntary and involuntary varieties of domination. Better to rely upon the indirect empowerment of enhanced competition and resourced exit—and to refuse to enforce marital contracts that are likely to trap unwilling partners, such as covenant marriage. With such policies in place, we can safely regard any dominating relationships as voluntary and therefore reject marital regulators as a paternalistic state intervention into the household.

Even if we set aside these worries about privacy and paternalism, however, we would still have good republican reasons to be suspicious of the idea of marital regulators. Remember that a republican state is tasked with minimizing *total* domination, be it private or public in nature, but the regulatory approach to direct empowerment would simply substitute the public domination of marital regulators for the private domination of abusive spouses. Because the powers of marital regulators will conflict with the interests of domineering husbands, households will have to be carefully monitored to ensure compliance. Regulators will therefore need broad powers to assess (via surprise inspections and video surveillance, say) and redress (by fines, jail time, or maybe just new or modified rules) the spousal abuse that silences women's voices. But such powers run the risk of increasing total domination, because dominating husbands will now be exposed to the same kind of arbitrary power they exercise over their own wives: marital regulators, given their wide remit to stop abuse, must be granted discretionary powers of a sort that can themselves be readily abused, especially given the complexity of their regulatory task and the limited ability of other state authorities to provide effective oversight due to that complexity. Regulators might use these powers to demand bribes from husbands in return for leniency or even to harass them as part of personal or ideological vendettas. Again, public domination does not require that these marital regulators actually abuse their positions—they may, in fact, be highly conscientious—but only requires that they have the *ability* to abuse, which they will certainly have given their broad powers of monitoring and enforcement.

These speculations about marital regulators may seem weirdly dystopian, like something out of the pages of Orwell or Zamyatin, but in fact they were perfectly common in medieval and early modern Europe: church officials, Catholic and Protestant alike, monitored and regulated the marital affairs of their congregants, with punishments ranging from excommunication to fines or even jail. Although officials did pay some attention to the welfare of vulnerable wives (including limited efforts to curb extreme marital violence—see Phillips 1988, 323–30), their primary focus was enforcing couples' obedience to the laws of church and state. For example, many legal codes at the time required married people to live together; if violations came to light, excommunication by the church or prosecution by the courts might result. Local church authorities were frequently called upon by superiors to monitor their congregants and report any failures to cohabit (Phillips 1988, 283–4). Even liberal Protestant reformers like Martin Bucer assumed that churches would play a central role in enforcing rules of conduct within marriage and admonishing violators, with the recalcitrant ones being handed over to civil courts (Phillips 1988, 71). Granted, most of these interventions had nothing to do with republican concerns regarding domination; in fact, many of them were intended to strengthen domination, be it of husbands over wives or of church and state over married couples. They nonetheless illustrate the dangers of handing wide regulatory powers over marriage to officialdom.[6]

Turning now to the participation option, we can see the same logic at work, leading to the same dangers. The democratic state can demand that domineering husbands include their wives in their decision-making processes, but because such inclusion is contrary to their interests, the state will again have to give regulators the necessary discretionary powers to monitor, assess, and redress spousal non-compliance. As we have just seen, though, such monitoring and enforcement powers can be abused by regulators, threatening an increase in total domination. Even if marital regulators stopped well short of requiring internal household democracy—for instance, they only required that husbands follow particular procedures before making important decisions, such as a waiting period prior to buying a house—the same concerns would arise. Again, state provision of resources to empower dependent wives offers a safer way to protect them from their domineering husbands than monitoring and enforcement efforts by marital regulators. Direct empowerment by state regulation is best limited to

---

[6] For a witty but frightening literary examination of clerical control over family life, see Kingsley Amis's alternate-history novel *The Alteration* (Amis 2013), in which Martin Luther becomes pope and religious authoritarianism has all of Europe in its grip.

extreme cases of abuse or to situations in which rational agency has been compromised in some way, a point to which I will return in the conclusion.[7]

Even if indirect empowerment is better than the direct kind at curtailing total domination within marriages, we may still worry about its side effects: domination is just one amongst many social evils, after all, and ameliorating it may exacerbate others. Religious conservatives are not alone, for instance, in their fear of family breakdown and social atomization more generally, and as we saw earlier on, they suspect that the very reforms that have eased marital exit over the past several decades have made these societal ills worse and that their principal victims have been the children of broken marriages. The evidence for this claim is fairly weak—as I noted earlier, there is an emerging consensus that no-fault divorce was a cause, but not a major one, of the increase in divorce rates and that its effect has faded of late (Allen and Gallagher 2007, 1)—but given the devastating costs of these ills, perhaps further efforts to enhance competition and resource exit in this domain are too risky.

A republican might be tempted to reply here that, given the unique evil of domination, we just have to accept these costs, however regretfully. I think a better reply, though, is that insofar as greater ease of marital exit has been a cause of these ills, this is due to an *insufficient* reduction in exit costs. The notion that doubling down on exit can simultaneously diminish domination and enhance social cohesion may seem outlandish, but consider the following: since the divorce peak of 1980, the divorce rate for college-educated women has not only been consistently lower than that for their non-college-educated peers but increasingly so—a somewhat surprising fact, given that their marital-exit costs should be lower due to better employment and spousal prospects and greater mobility (Isen and Stevenson 2010). There are a number of possible explanations for this result, including selection effects (maybe the characteristics that make one more likely to finish a college degree also make one less likely to divorce) and the fact that college-educated women search longer for a spouse, improving matching. I strongly suspect that there is another factor at work here, though: a more egalitarian marriage culture among the educated, one that has resulted in part from credible threats of exit by educated wives with ever-increasing bargaining

---

[7] I will pass over the third, privatization option in the main text, though I do want to mention here the possibility that women might act jointly, formally or informally, to counter masculine collusion. For instance, consider the Japanese phenomenon of so-called "parasite singles" (*parasaito shinguru*), especially young women, who continue to live at home with their parents while they hold down jobs, indulge in consumerism, and postpone marriage and childbirth (Lunsing 2003). One might view this as an informal but collective response to the continued patriarchal nature of the Japanese family, in which wives are expected to quit their jobs upon giving birth to take care of children and elderly parents. It might also give us a partial explanation for why Japan has one of the world's lowest fertility rates (Central Intelligence Agency 2014).

power. As I argued in Chapter 1, if the threat of exit is credible and the abusive parties therefore yield, the threat will not have to be exercised, i.e., no exit will occur, and this can be true even if the threat is entirely implicit, a background condition created by the shifting advantages and disadvantages of the participants. Ever-lower exit costs for educated women have allowed them to redefine the culture of elite marriage, forcing men to accept relationships built on equality and mutual respect and stabilizing their marriages in the process.[8]

There is no reason for such beneficial changes to continue to be limited to those of higher socioeconomic status, however. By enhancing competition and resourcing exit for less-educated dependent wives, we can put them in a position to bargain for better marital conditions. Even if a largely formal marital freedom has made them vulnerable to divorce threats by abusive husbands and even dissuaded others from marrying at all, leaving intact an inegalitarian marital subculture, a more substantive marital freedom could help spread elite-marriage values throughout the entire society.[9] If this were to happen, we might have reason to hope that Montaigne's idealized portrait of Roman marriage could actually be realized in our own society:

We thought we were tying our marriage-knots more tightly by removing all means of undoing them; but the tighter we pulled the knot of constraint the looser and slacker became the knot of our will and affection. In Rome, on the contrary, what made marriages honoured and secure for so long a period was freedom to break them at will. Men loved their wives more because they could lose them; and during a period when anyone was quite free to divorce, more than five hundred years went by before a single one did so. (Montaigne 1993, 698)

The Limits and Potential of Marital Freedom

I have argued in this chapter that the indirect empowerment of women's voices through greater competition and resourced exit in marriage and labor markets is the safest, most effective way to check the arbitrary exercise of power within the family, i.e., marital freedom is antipower in the domestic sphere. As I indicated above, though, there are circumstances in which this mode of protection will

---

[8] Some evidence for this process at work is provided by a recent Pew Research Center report. In 1965, for example, wives did four times as much child care, eight times as much housework, and less than one-fifth as much paid work as their husbands, working a total of two hours per week *more* than they did; by 2011, they were doing only twice as much child care, 80 percent more housework, and a bit over half as much paid work, working a total of one hour per week *less* than they did (Pew Research Center 2013, 1). Such convergence is even more striking within elite marriages.

[9] This kind of top-down cultural diffusion has occurred in numerous other historical contexts: see, for example, Elias 1983 and Clark 2007.

prove inadequate. For example, when wives have been subjected to systematic psychological, physical, and/or sexual abuse, their rational agency may be compromised (Walker 2006). Because marital freedom presumes such agency—without it, wives will lack the ability to hold their husbands accountable and defend their own interests through voice or exit—alternative means will have to be found to protect them, including monitoring of households and the kind of mandatory-arrest policies encouraged by the 1994 Violence Against Women Act (Cho and Wilke 2005). In the end, we may be unable to avoid augmenting indirect empowerment with the direct kind when abuse becomes severe enough to threaten women's agential capacities.[10]

I should also concede the difficulty, or even the impossibility, of extending my preferred approach to household dependents, including minor children and even elderly parents. Children will generally lack the rational agency that is needed to exercise exit responsibly, though as they approach majority they may be able to exit via emancipation by the courts; in their earlier years, exit will be possible only through a transfer of custody, whether initiated by the parents or state authorities. As a result, they will have to rely upon the moral constraints governing their parents' behavior and the legal interventions of the state *in extremis* (e.g., in cases of neglect or violence) to escape the arbitrary exercise of parental authority (Ferejohn 2001, 82). For dependent elderly parents, the situation is far more complex. If they are mentally incompetent, their condition may resemble that of minor children. If they are mentally competent, on the other hand, exit may be a real option, especially when alternatives are abundant (e.g., other relatives, elder-care facilities) and exit is financially viable due to private savings or state aid; again, effective competition and resourced exit are key here. When these conditions are absent, though, direct empowerment may be required, whether in the form of the regulation option (monitoring and supervision by relevant state authorities) or the participation option (e.g., enforcing the rights of the elderly to have some say in particular aspects of their care). Whether marital freedom can become a model for familial freedom more broadly, then, is doubtful: protecting household dependents from domination will frequently require direct empowerment of voice in one form or another.[11]

---

[10] Might patriarchal subcultures similarly degrade their agential capacities? Such false-consciousness claims usually smack of paternalism, and as I argued earlier, many attractive alternatives to the regulation option are available here.

[11] Domination of dependents can be surprisingly indirect. For example, failure to take proper account of the interests of future generations when we deliberate about government deficits or environmental preservation might constitute a kind of intergenerational domination: see Bohman 2011 on this point.

As I will argue in the following chapters, however, marital freedom *can* serve as a model in many other contexts. Whether we consider the domination of workers by abusive managers or that of businesses by corrupt regulators and politicians, the kinds of policy instruments that were used to limit marital power through resourced exit and enhanced competition can also be used to limit market and political power. Marital freedom, in short, can act as a template for both market and political freedoms—and by doing so, it can offer a fresh approach to combating domination, one that is less dependent on social-democratic interventions than on empowered choice and free mobility in labor and locational markets. As we shall see, John Milton's divorcive conception of freedom promises us liberation well beyond the domestic sphere.

3

Market

Republicanism, though characterized throughout its history by certain core beliefs and anxieties (e.g., an emphasis on active citizenship, a commitment to the separation of powers and the rule of law, and an ongoing concern with political venality), has been a diverse political tradition, especially in its assessment of commercial society. Consider, for instance, the near-contemporary republican authors Jean-Jacques Rousseau and Adam Smith.[1] Rousseau wrote approvingly of the ancient Romans' "contempt for commerce" and condemned "pecuniary interest" as "the worst of all [interests], the vilest, the most liable to corruption" (Rousseau 1997, 131, 226). His hostility to a monetized economy with its complex division of labor even extended to tax payments as a substitute for *corvées*:

> It is the hustle and bustle of commerce and the arts, it is the avid interest in gain, it is softness and love of comforts that change personal services [to the state] into money. One gives up a portion of one's profit in order to increase it at leisure. Give money, and soon you will have chains. The word *finance* is a slave's word.... In a truly free State the citizens will do everything with their hands and nothing with money: Far from paying to be exempted from their duties, they would pay to fulfill it themselves. (Rousseau 1997, 113)

Smith, by contrast, was not particularly disturbed by the fact that "it is not from the benevolence of the butcher, the brewer, or the baker, that we expect our dinner, but from their regard to their own interest.... As it is by treaty, by barter, and by purchase, that we obtain from one another the greater part of those mutual good offices which we stand in need of, so it is this same trucking disposition which originally gives occasion to the division of labor" (Smith

---

[1] See Hanley (2008) and Rasmussen (2008) for a more systematic comparison of these two thinkers on the topic of commercial society and Rousselière (2016) on Rousseau's specific views. For a broader history of republicanism's conflicted attitude towards markets, see MacGilvray (2011). Last, I should note that Pettit himself seems to question Rousseau's republican credentials: "to those in the older republican tradition—for example, to Machiavelli or to Harrington—Rousseau's vision would have appeared to celebrate a form of dependency on the will of the corporate whole—in effect, the will of the majority—at odds with a vision of freedom as non-domination" (2014, 12).

1981, 26–7 [I.ii.2–3]). Far from regarding the "hustle and bustle of commerce" as slavery's prelude, he saw competitive markets as a source of liberation from feudal dependence: the modern "tradesman or artificer," he pointed out, "derives his subsistence from the employment, not of one, but of a hundred or a thousand different customers. Though in some measure obliged to them all, therefore, he is not absolutely dependent upon any one of them" (Smith 1981, 420 [III.iv.12]; Herzog 2016, 55–7). Whereas Rousseau saw the market order as a deadly threat to republican values, Smith viewed it as an essential tool for their realization.

The recent revival of the republican political tradition raises anew this debated question of how republicans should regard the market economy. Critics of this revivalist republicanism, such as Gerald Gaus, have insisted that it is "profoundly antimarket.... [In it,] the market is almost totally delegitimized" (Gaus 2003, 68), in effect pegging Pettit and other neo-republicans as Rousseauean enemies of commercial society. According to Gaus, Pettit believes that "markets are always a clear threat to [republican] freedom" because:

> unless checked... differential success at accumulating resources always involves domination. The wealthy always *could* use their resources to dominate others. Indeed, for Pettit all market competition is a form of interference—"I interfere with you if I destroy your custom by deliberately undercutting your prices." Thus, an entrepreneur who *could* destroy his rivals' custom by cutting prices appears to dominate his competition. (Gaus 2003, 68–9)[2]

If all that is required to dominate others is simply the potential to interfere, Gaus suggests, then republican opposition to market competition and the economic inequalities that frequently result from it is assured.

Republicans such as Richard Dagger and Pettit himself have firmly pushed back against this characterization. Dagger, for example, notes that "the ability to engage in free exchanges in the marketplace enables people to be self-governing," a republican desideratum (Dagger 2006, 158). For his part, Pettit approvingly mentions Adam Smith's belief that "far from threatening republican freedom, the market could reduce dependency and domination" (Pettit 2006b, 142). This being said, republican support for markets can at times have a half-hearted quality to it. Dagger grudgingly concedes that there is "at least... nothing immoral" about free exchange and that "markets are fine in their place," but he simultaneously emphasizes the need to "protect communities against the ravages

---

[2] The internal quote is from Pettit 1997, 54. Pettit indicates in the very same paragraph that such interference may be "morally impeccable," and as we shall see shortly, he later argues that under competitive conditions, at least, such undercutting does not count as "arbitrary interference," the republican *summum malum* (Pettit 1997, 205).

of market competition," a concern to which I will return later in the chapter (Dagger 2006, 158, 163). In a similar manner, Pettit writes of a justifiable republican "complacency" towards even idealized market exchanges rather than enthusiasm for them, and at times he treats economists' arguments for competition skeptically, even dismissively, describing them with such terms as "allegedly" and "so it is argued" and at one point calling them a "sort of magic" (Pettit 1997, 203, 225, 2006b, 142). Granted, these are frequently matters of tone rather than substance, but they are consistent features of republican texts, and they are noticed by critics such as Gaus.

In this chapter, I will argue that the proper republican attitude toward competitive markets is celebratory, not acquiescent, and that republicanism demands such markets for precisely the same reason that it demands the rule of law: because both are essential institutions for protecting individuals from arbitrary interference. A system of competitive markets achieves an economic constitutionalism that parallels the more familiar political constitutionalism of the separation of powers, bicameralism, federalism, bills of rights, and judicial review. To be more specific, I will show how economic competition restrains—and in the limit, eradicates—market power and how such restraint helps us realize "market freedom," i.e., freedom as non-domination in the context of economic exchange. I believe this extension of republican thinking into exchange relations is consistent with both the spirit and the letter of contemporary republican theories, especially that of Philip Pettit, and I will make continuous reference to them throughout the chapter. I intend this, in short, to be a friendly amendment to contemporary republicanism, one that will enhance its appeal in certain quarters (e.g., among economists) without compromising any of its fundamental normative commitments.

This amendment will have the additional benefit of buttressing republicanism against the charge (made by Christopher McMahon, among others) that it is insufficiently determinate with respect to its policy implications (McMahon 2005; cf. Pettit 2006a). Pettit in particular has perhaps made himself vulnerable to such charges by suggesting, for example, that "there is not much of interest that can be said about republican economic policy in the abstract" (Pettit 1997, 163). I hope to show here that an abstract commitment to competitive markets follows quite readily from contemporary republicanism and that it generates a variety of policy implications regarding labor-market reform, antitrust, basic income, capitalist demogrants, etc. Some of these policies will be ones that republicans themselves have advocated, while others will be new to republicanism and at times might require republicans to revise some of their economic-policy preconceptions.

I should note that a "celebratory" attitude towards markets does not necessarily imply a commitment to libertarian or even classical-liberal policies. Market freedom requires effective competition, and only the state can secure many of its regulatory and institutional preconditions. More specifically, the republican economic model that I will argue for in this chapter will resemble a modified version of a common European social model, viz. the Nordic model, which combines flexible labor markets (including ease of hiring and firing), free trade, and bracing competition with high levels of social support in the form of generous welfare benefits and job retraining; the Danish variant of this model is sometimes called "flexicurity."[3] One problem with this model, however, is that it tolerates both strong unions and employers' associations, then depends upon their mutual restraint—grace in the exercise of their economic power—to preserve flexible labor markets. As I will also argue, this tolerance is inconsistent with republicanism, which demands an aggressive, Anglo-Saxon approach to competition policy in all markets, including labor markets; republican economics rejects the halfway house of "reciprocal power" in favor of purging power from economic relations. The resulting hybrid, which one might call the "Anglo-Nordic" model, is the key to realizing freedom as non-domination in the context of economic exchange.

I will begin this chapter by exploring the meaning of market power, using labor markets as a case in point. Concentrations of power on either side of the market (be it monopoly, monopsony, or less extreme forms) make exploitation, discrimination, and domination possible; introducing effective competition in such contexts helps promote market freedom, understood as non-domination in exchange relations. In the following section, I will argue that market freedom is itself a kind of antipower on Pettit's own understanding of the term; I then go on to show that Pettit and other republicans anticipate this result in their own writings. I conclude the chapter with some further reflections on the limits of exit as a tool for curbing market domination as well as on how my findings extend and reorient republican theory.

Market Power versus Market Freedom

As we saw in Chapter 1, market power gives leeway for exploitation, discrimination, and domination. To clarify these concepts, I will focus first on a labor-market example—specifically, a labor market having a single employer. (Anaconda

---

[3] For a discussion of the four canonical European social models (viz. Mediterranean, Continental, Nordic, and Anglo-Saxon), see Sapir (2006).

Copper Mining Company, which dominated the labor market of Butte, Montana, during the late nineteenth and twentieth centuries, roughly approximated such a labor monopsonist—see Mercier 2001.) First, a successful labor monopsonist will exploit its workers: it will hire workers up to but not beyond the point where the marginal revenue product of labor (i.e., the contribution to a firm's revenues by the last worker hired) just equals the marginal expense (i.e., the cost of hiring that last worker *plus* the additional labor costs associated with raising the wage of existing workers to the new, higher level required to attract the last worker [assuming uniform wage rates]); under monopsony conditions, though, this will typically result in a wage rate that is less than the marginal revenue product of labor, meaning that workers as a group fail to be paid according to their (marginal) contribution to the firm's revenues, as they would under genuinely competitive labor-market conditions (Nicholson 1995, 724–8). This is *exploitation* in the neoclassical sense of the term. The firm might pay its workers more than this monopsony wage rate, but it would do so as a kind of discretionary charity, adding insult to the injury of exploitation.

The previous paragraph assumed a uniform wage rate, i.e., all workers (of the same skill level) being paid an identical wage rate. If the monopsonist had perfect information about each worker's reservation wage (i.e., the lowest wage at which he or she would be willing to work), however, it could practice perfect wage *discrimination*, paying each worker no more than his or her reservation wage. Monopsonists are rarely omniscient in this way, however, so their attempts at wage discrimination will be imperfect: e.g., they will have to segment the workforce according to certain readily observable characteristics (like race, gender, or age) that have been found to correlate with the wage elasticity of labor supply (i.e., the responsiveness of workers to changes in wage rates) and pay lower wages to parts of the labor force that are relatively unresponsive to wage cuts (Nicholson 1995, 728–9).

Finally, unless the monopsonistic firm can practice perfect wage discrimination (which is extremely unlikely), it will be driven by the profit motive to employ fewer workers than it would under competitive conditions and thereby to generate unemployment: unhired workers, after all, have no alternative employers to whom to turn. Those workers fortunate enough to be employed, however, are placed in a highly precarious, vulnerable position, as they also have no alternative employers to whom they can turn and are therefore subject to the caprice of the monopsonist and his managers. This absence of meaningful exit options for workers makes them liable to arbitrary exercises of economic power, i.e., *domination*. Some aspects of this power we have already seen: the discretionary power of the firm to pay above the monopsony wage rate as a form of charity (underwritten by monopsony rents, ironically) and to practice wage discrimination according to morally irrelevant criteria. Other aspects are much darker, as the early history of industrialization suggests, including sexual exploitation and other forms of physical abuse (e.g., denial of lunch or bathroom breaks, abysmal health and safety conditions, even beatings).

Such are the bitter fruits of labor monopsony, which is market power in possibly its most extreme and disturbing form—a fact that has not gone unnoticed by some republicans. Pettit, for example, in the midst of selling republicanism's virtues to socialists, describes Marx's belief that workers are:

> wage slaves... dependent on the grace and mercy of their employer... [and] exposed to the possibility of arbitrary interference.... If the employers in any area are *collectively* capable of blacklisting someone who displeases them, as many nineteenth-century employers certainly were, and if unemployment effectively means destitution, then it is clear why socialists should have thought that workers were nothing more than wage slaves. (Pettit 1997, 141 [emphasis added]; cf. Pettit 2006b, 142, 2007, 5)

In this passage, Pettit illustrates that if an area's employers act as a collective monopsonist, i.e., a labor-purchasing cartel, then they can dominate their wage-slave employees, just as Marx claims, and thereby deprive them of their (republican) freedom. To advance freedom as non-domination, the state must combat such exercises of labor-market power—whether carried out by individual monopsonists or employer cartels—by antitrust action and other policy interventions, including what Pettit describes as the "discipline of nondiscrimination" in wage setting (Pettit 2006b, 142, 145 ["legislate against monopolies"]).

Labor monopsony may be market power at its most extreme, but it is also relatively rare. Less extreme forms of market power on the employer side, however, are more common (Bhaskar et al. 2002). The most studied example is probably the market for hospital nurses. Even in metropolitan areas, the number of hospitals may be relatively small; moreover, these hospitals often practice what they euphemistically call "wage standardization" (i.e., oligopsonistic collusion). Collusion of this sort, be it explicit or tacit, gives individual hospitals substantial market power, a power heightened by other market features (e.g., differentiation of hospitals by location, safety records, etc.). As with monopsonists, this market power gives individual hospitals the ability to drive wages below the marginal revenue product of labor, practice various forms of discrimination, etc. (Sullivan 1989). Any degree of market power may offer opportunities for not just exploitation and discrimination but domination as well and may therefore justify policy responses of the kind mentioned above.

At the opposite extreme from monopsonistic labor markets (with oligopsonistic as well as monopsonistically-competitive labor markets filling the space between) are perfectly competitive labor markets. These markets are characterized by both large numbers of (potential) employers and workers and frictionless exit from employment relationships. Under these conditions, neither employers nor workers will have the capacity to manipulate wages; as economists would put it, they will be price-takers, not price-makers. More specifically, competition among employers and workers will drive wages into equality with the marginal revenue product of labor for each grade of labor: any employer who attempts to pay less than this competitive wage will lose his workers to another firm; any worker who tries to claim more will be replaced by another equally-skilled worker. As a result, neoclassical exploitation will be eliminated, as will discrimination: no firm will be in a position to pay lower wages to some segments of the workforce on grounds unrelated to productivity, as other firms would simply bid their wages back up. Finally, no firm will be in a position to dominate workers, given the possibility of costless exit: as Pettit himself points out, "in a well-functioning labor market ... no one would depend on any particular master and so no one would be at the mercy of a master: he or she could move on to employment elsewhere in the event of suffering arbitrary interference."[4]

Given these valuable features of competitive labor markets, what public policies will best promote them? First, we should note that many existing public policies undermine competition in labor markets; thus, promotion of competition will require us to abolish or reform these policies. For example, closed-shop unionism and related "for cause" dismissal clauses in labor contracts create market power for workers, making it harder for employers to hire and replace workers at competitive wages and discouraging hiring. A move to right-to-work laws and universal at-will employment would reduce these labor-market frictions. Also, though private-sector union power has waned substantially since World War II, it has been replaced by an equally anti-competitive proliferation of occupational licensing rules: in the 1950s, a mere 5 percent of workers required state licenses, but now 35 percent do; by cartelizing professions ranging from hairdressing and cosmetology to horse massaging and bartending, licensing has made possible the exclusion of competitors, the exploitation of consumers, and wage rates 18 percent higher *ceteris paribus* than those in unlicensed professions (Kleiner and Krueger 2013). One example of the kind of exploitation and domination that licensing rules enable is the relationship between dentists and dental hygienists, which bears a striking similarity to the hospital/nurse relationship discussed earlier: state licensing rules that require dental hygienists to be

---

[4] Pettit 2006b, 142; cf. Lovett 2009, 820: "in a theoretically perfect market, all entries and exits would be costless; it follows that, since no one would be dependent on anyone else, there'd be no domination under these conditions."

employed and supervised by dentists result in higher earnings for dentists and lower earnings (and employment) for hygienists relative to markets where hygienists can work independently (Kleiner 2013, ch. 6). Shifting from licensing to a less exclusionary screening process (e.g., state certification) would retain most of the health and safety benefits of licensing without undermining labor-market competition (Friedman 1962, ch. 9).

Another worry about licensing policies and similar anti-competitive interventions is that they may slow domination-curbing developments in technology and business structure. Consider, for instance, how historic advances in communications, computing power, and search algorithms have made it possible to match tasks to workers in ways that circumvent hierarchically-organized firms. The most prominent example is the creation of Uber, Lyft, and Sidecar to match riders to drivers and bypass traditional taxi companies; by permitting drivers to be independent operators, they free them from potential domination within these firms. Private taxi firms, though, currently benefit from city licensing requirements (e.g., New York City's infamous medallion system) that enable them to cartelize cab services and exploit both drivers and riders, and they are suing Uber and other online platforms in order to protect their monopoly profits (Dompe and Smith 2014). Here again, unwise public policies stymie competition and inadvertently facilitate domination.

Many public policies, of course, can and do encourage competition. I discussed antitrust action and related interventions (e.g., non-discrimination rules) above, which make labor markets more competitive by either increasing the number of competing employers or forcing incumbent employers to behave in a more competitive manner (by, say, breaking up cartel arrangements). Recent revelations that Google, Apple, Intel, and Adobe colluded in a scheme not to solicit one another's employees are a case in point; the resulting class-action suit is leading to an antitrust settlement of hundreds of millions of dollars for the exploited engineers (Streitfeld 2014). Also, state agencies might educate employees about their contractual rights and collect and disseminate information about other job opportunities, be they local or national: ignorance can be a friction in its own right, leading workers to stay in employment relations they would be better off leaving (Viscusi 1983, 156–62; cf. Pettit 1997, 159: "ignorance of relevant standards and expectations").

More radically, the state might pursue redistributive policies to make it easier for workers to exit workplaces. Workers may have a tough time, for example, saving up the money necessary to move to another place in search of work—an especially pressing problem in impoverished and insular regions of the country like rural Appalachia (Lowrey 2014). Governments could provide "relocation vouchers" to enable just such moves, tightening local labor markets and disciplining abusive employers in the process. The Trade Adjustment Assistance program already offers such help to displaced workers in the form of moving allowances and stipendiary support to take up a job in a new city; unemployment insurance could be changed to allow the long-term unemployed to take advances on their benefits for the purposes of a move (Moretti 2012). In a similar fashion, states could empower workers to seek alternative employment—including self-employment—by offering "capitalist" demogrants, i.e., seed money to encourage the accumulation of physical, financial, and human capital; these might come in the form of small-business awards, start-up cash for playing the stock market or buying an annuity to subsidize a low-paying but rewarding career (e.g., topiary gardening), educational vouchers, etc. Finally, as certain republicans have proposed, the state might deliver an unconditional basic income, which would serve as a firm backstop against employment exploitation, discrimination, and domination by making it possible for workers to exit the labor market entirely (Pettit 2007; Lovett 2009, 825–8).

Up until now, I have focused exclusively on labor markets, but market power can lead to exploitation, discrimination, and domination in other sorts of markets as well, all of which can be countered by the introduction of effective competition. Consider, for example, Dagger's example of someone whose "apples are the only available source of food" and who consequently has an "effective monopoly on that good"; as he points out, this will create a form of dependency that is inconsistent with freedom as non-domination (Dagger 2006, 158). Policy interventions analogous to those surveyed above can remedy this situation by recreating competitive conditions or at least requiring market actors to behave in competitive ways, for as Pettit rightly argues:

> short of great differences in bargaining power, this arrangement does not mean that anyone is exposed to the possibility of arbitrary interference by any other or any group of others. One seller may be able to interfere with another by undercutting the other's price, but the second should be free, above the level of the competitive price, to undercut that price in turn; thus there is no question of permanent exposure to interference. (Pettit 1997, 205; *pace* Gaus 2003, 68)

As Pettit suggests, and as I will argue more explicitly in the next section, economic competition restrains—and in the limit, eradicates—market power and helps us to realize "market freedom," i.e., freedom as non-domination in the context of economic exchange.

Market Freedom as Antipower

Competitive markets are antipower in the precise sense spelled out by Pettit: specifically, in perfectly competitive markets, participants have no capacity to interfere with impunity and at will with the economic interests of other participants.

They enjoy no capacity to interfere at will because market prices are set by impersonal forces of supply and demand, so there is no room for discretionary price setting, i.e., arbitrary exercises of market power. Any attempt to deviate from this competitive price (by, say, overcharging consumers or underpaying workers) will lead to the loss of trade and the punishment of reduced profits; hence, they also have no capacity to interfere with impunity. These features of competitive markets are antipower not just in Pettit's procedural sense but in his substantive sense as well, because they "track the interests" of the participants in at least one important way: under certain conditions, perfect competition will generate a welfare optimum, securing productive and allocative efficiency and thereby making the economic pie as large as possible—a result that is in the interest of all participants, differ as they may on how that pie should be divided up.[5]

Another way to see how competitive markets are antipower is to notice their quality of, to use Pettit's terminology, "non-manipulability." Pettit uses this term to describe a certain feature of institutional "instruments" (e.g., public law) employed by the republican state:

Designed to further certain public ends, they should be maximally resistant to being deployed on an arbitrary, perhaps sectional, basis. No one individual or group should have discretion in how the instruments are used.... The institutions and initiatives involved should not allow of manipulation at anyone's individual whim. (Pettit 1997, 173)

He then proceeds to lay out "three broad conditions that a non-manipulable system will need to satisfy." I'll describe them one by one, showing how competitive markets meet them and thereby embody an economic constitutionalism parallel to the political kind that is Pettit's chief concern:

1. **Empire-of-law condition:** This condition demands that political power be exercised in a manner consistent with the rule of law, i.e., laws "should be general and apply to everyone, including the legislators themselves; they should be promulgated and made known in advance to those to whom they apply; they should be intelligible, consistent, and not subject to constant change; and so on" (Pettit 1997, 174). Prices in a competitive market meet some of these conditions, as they are general, apply to everyone, and are public in nature (transparent). To be sure, they are subject to constant change and are obviously not "promulgated," being the product of a spontaneous order rather than an organization, but they otherwise resemble

---

[5] For a proof of this claim (the First Welfare Theorem) and the conditions under which it will hold, see Debreu 1959.

an economic rule of law, one that keeps the market from becoming "a playground for the arbitrary will" of its participants (Pettit 1997, 174).

2. **Dispersion-of-power condition:** This condition requires that "powers which officials have under any regime of law should be dispersed" by familiar mechanisms such as the separation of powers, bicameralism, federalism, and international legalism (Pettit 1997, 177–80). This condition is readily met by competitive markets because they are characterized by a large number of (potential) buyers and sellers, which in combination with the other features of such markets (e.g., perfect information, free exit) turns all participants into price-takers rather than price-makers. Under perfect competition, at least, economic power is not so much dispersed as extinguished.

3. **Counter-majoritarian condition:** This condition insists that laws be insulated from "excessively easy, majoritarian change" (Pettit 1997, 180). In competitive markets, no group of buyers or sellers—including majorities of either—is in a position to exercise arbitrary power. The "tyranny of the majority" is ruled out, as is every other sort of economic tyranny.

This proposed analogy between economic and political constitutionalism is admittedly imperfect. One important difference, already mentioned above, is that the "economic law" of a competitive price is not "promulgated" in any sense and therefore would "background, not foreground, reason": i.e., competitive prices are not the product of any reasoned democratic deliberation but rather an emergent property of a certain type of economic order (Pettit 1997, 203, cf. 224–5). Such backgrounding is essential, of course, given the staggering complexity of the economic task that is involved and the gross inadequacy of central planning as an alternative solution—even if such planning were deliberative and democratic in nature—but the disanalogy nevertheless remains. Also, the notion that freedom as non-domination is achieved in a perfectly competitive market because its participants are powerless, individually and collectively, to shape something as socially consequential as prices might strike some readers as less of a realization of republicanism than a *reductio* of it.

Still, it would be a mistake to make too much of this disanalogy, as the republican state itself requires some measure of such backgrounding owing to the complexity of its own task. For example, administrative efficiency will often require that state agents be permitted "a substantial degree of discretion," lest we forego "all possibility of fitting government action to the needs of particular cases," yet such discretion is unlikely to be wholly guided by democratic public reason and may only with some difficulty even be constrained by it (Pettit 1997, 175–6).

Perhaps even more to the point, a republican state may decide to make conscious use of mechanisms, such as lotteries to assign spots in charter schools, that leave allocative decisions to chance. So long as they meet certain conditions—e.g., reflective public endorsement, fair and impartial supervision, and the promotion of the common good—such mechanisms are surely unobjectionable. I would contend that competitive markets are similar mechanisms: so long as democratic political organs sanction them as mutually advantageous (if individually risky), set up their legal and institutional preconditions (e.g., property, contract, and tort as elements of the private law), and maintain their competitive nature over time (through antitrust and the various forms of redistribution catalogued above), these markets can be understood as legislative products of a democratic will— even if the vagaries of the price system are as little under *direct* democratic control as the motion of balls in a lottery machine. From a republican perspective, the important question to ask about markets is whether they protect their participants from arbitrary interference and track their interests in both a substantive sense (improving their life prospects) and a procedural one (submitting to both their endorsement and their supervision through a democratic political process). Competitive markets, at least, can meet these conditions and therefore realize freedom as non-domination.

One objection that could be raised to my account so far is that free exit and the associated conditions of perfect competition might sometimes fail to hold and are consequently inadequate guarantors of non-domination. Nien-hê Hsieh, for example, argues that "as an alternative to exit, workers need to be able to exercise voice—to have the capacity to express dissent without exiting," which can be achieved if the state "provides workers with the right to contest decisions within the context of the decision-making process internal to economic enterprises" (Hsieh 2005, 134; cf. Dagger 2006, 163). Consider the Anaconda Copper Mining example with which I began the last section. Perhaps at that time and place, government efforts to promote competitive labor markets—by antitrust action, laws against wage discrimination, and the provision of information, travel grants, capitalist demogrants, and/or an unconditional basic income for all workers— were either economically or politically infeasible. Under those conditions, the best way to secure non-domination might have been to empower workers' voices by, for example, encouraging not just unionization but the "narrowly defined job descriptions" and other varieties of worker protection (from "for cause" dismissal clauses to German-style "co-determination") that unions frequently demand (Hsieh 2005, 135). In short, the regulation, participation, and privatization options that I surveyed in Chapter 1 must remain on the table if we are to be serious about curbing domination.

While Hsieh is surely right to question whether an *"exclusive* reliance on the right to exit" is sufficient under all circumstances to prevent workplace domination, "voice" carries substantial risks of *increasing* domination and should therefore remain an exception to the rule of promoting free exit and effective competition. Lovett, for instance, points out that "workplace regulations" and other attempts to "regulate...social relationships," while perhaps useful for stopping certain "gross abuses," may in the end simply substitute one form of domination for another:

> There will always be discovered new and ever-more subtle means of converting material advantage into domination. In the long run it is unlikely that public policy could ever keep pace with, much less anticipate, such innovations—except perhaps with a regulatory structure so dense and intrusive as to raise serious objections on other grounds. (For starters, a state powerful enough to accomplish this task might itself become a great source of domination.)   (Lovett 2009, 825–6)

In contrast to intrusive workplace monitoring and intervention, government delivery of resources that empower workers in labor-market choices can remain largely aloof from relations within the firm, trusting instead that free exit will discipline owners and managers and prevent them from dominating their employees.[6] To be certain, discretionary power over workers will continue to be exercised by owners and their managers, as such discretion (e.g., in task assignment) is essential to maintaining a flexible and efficient production process, but state empowerment of workers via antitrust action, resource transfers, etc., will put them in a position to choose from among a menu of workplaces that differ by kind and degree of managerial discretion exercised inter alia. Such choice—including the limit choice of wholly exiting the labor market, which is made possible by capitalist demogrants or an unconditional basic income—guarantees that this residual managerial discretion is non-arbitrary, as it "tracks the interests...of the person suffering the interference."[7] These choices will typically involve tradeoffs (e.g., less discretion might mean lower wages), but so long as workers have been empowered in the ways I described, such tradeoffs can reasonably be viewed as tracking their interests.

Arguing otherwise has the weird implication that when I decide to order *omakase* (chef's choice) at a sushi restaurant, I thereby problematically expose

---

[6] As with the intervention of marital regulators into family affairs, worries about privacy and paternalism arise here, too, though presumably with less force. Protecting privacy and preventing regulatory paternalism on the job enable modes of communication and cooperation that transform participants into self-governing agents in economic as well as political life, both of which are republican desiderata. See Roberts (2014) for a more extended discussion.

[7] Pettit 1997, 55; also, see my Chapter 2 discussion of Pettit's "substantive" sense of power.

myself to (potential) arbitrary interference. So long as I have a broad array of affordable culinary options—set menus, chef's choice at other eateries, dining at home, etc.—my choice of *omakase* suggests that the discretion consequently exercised is not arbitrary (assuming that it stays within mutually understood limits, of course: e.g., I am not served a burrito). My decision to submit to the bounded discretion of a sushi chef is analogous to the decision (discussed earlier) of a democratic people to submit to the bounded "discretion" of lotteries or competitive markets: if such submission tracks their interests in both (1) substantive and (2) procedural ways, then the subsequent exercise of discretion does not constitute arbitrary interference. In the sushi case, my interests are tracked if (1) I anticipate benefiting from the discretion (i.e., the price plus the risks of being disappointed are outweighed by the expected benefits of surprise and gustatory satisfaction) and (2) I have exit options in case I do not benefit, and chef's discretion is bounded by mutually understood norms. The same logic applies to employment: when I submit to managerial discretion by accepting a job, subsequent exercises of such discretion are not arbitrary if (1) I anticipate benefiting from it (i.e., the wages I receive outweigh the expected unpleasantness of being ordered around and having to do tiresome tasks) and (2) I have numerous exit options in case I do not benefit, and managerial discretion is circumscribed by mutually understood customary and contractual rules. As a result, arbitrariness within employment relations can—at least in principle—be prevented without intrusive state monitoring and intervention in workplaces, which itself threatens domination.

Unfortunately, the dangers of relying upon voice are not necessarily reduced by replacing state power with non-state (e.g., union) power: fighting fire with fire still risks burning everyone involved. This is apparently why Pettit dislikes what he calls the "reciprocal power" strategy for achieving non-domination, which involves countering private power with private power (Pettit 1997, 67–8). In the labor market, for example, it may require countering the market power of a monopsonist with that of a union monopolist; such a "bilateral monopoly" will restrain discretion but leave wage determination to the relative bargaining power of the two sides (Nicholson 1995, 729–30). Pettit's understandable concern with such a solution is that by it "arbitrary interference and domination may be reduced, but it is not ever going to be eliminated," because the residual mutual interference involved fails to "track the interests and ideas of those who are affected" (Pettit 1997, 67). Even worse, systematic government efforts to enhance the market power of one side against the other may have the (net) effect of increasing domination. For example, the National Labor Relations Act, by protecting the ability of workers to organize and collectively bargain, may have reduced domination in those areas or industries in which the employer side was monopsonistic or oligopsonistic but increased it in those in which it was competitive: monopolistic unions, just like monopsonistic employers, have enormous power to exploit, discriminate against, and dominate the weaker side—in this case, unorganized firms. Consider the case of public (non-tertiary) education in the USA. Here, a vast number of individual school districts compete for an educated, relatively mobile teacher population; hence, the employer side is reasonably competitive. The employee side, on the other hand, has oligopolistic characteristics: teachers' unions are organized at local, state, and even national levels (under the umbrellas of the National Education Association and the American Federation of Teachers) and coordinate their activities across school districts and states. If there is market power here, it is mostly on the educator side—an advantage made possible in large part by collective-bargaining rights for public employees. If freedom is antipower, as Pettit argues, then market power must be countered and if possible eliminated wherever it arises, and this commitment will usually mean that the state should limit its market interventions to promoting free exit and active competition.

A similarly skeptical perspective on unions can be found throughout Pettit's writings. He sometimes expresses concerns about union power, as when he asks us to "think of the case of small entrepreneurs who are held to ransom by the primary or secondary picketing of a powerful trade union that can put them out of business" (2014, 91). When he lauds unions, it is invariably within the context of monopsonistic or oligopsonistic labor markets and is generally historical in nature (e.g., Pettit 1997, 95 ["industrial world of the nineteenth century"], 141–2 ["nineteenth-century employers"]). Additionally, he tends to favor exit over voice as a means of dealing with domination; for example, he states that "other protections, such as those that strong trade unions may provide, are possible against such alien control [i.e., oligopsony]. But the most effective of all protections, and one that should complement other measures available, would be one's ability to leave employment and fall back on a basic wage available unconditionally from the state" (Pettit 2007, 5). Finally, as the Pettit quotation at the close of the last section shows, one seller undercutting another seller's price, which may lead to a painful loss of trade, does not qualify as arbitrary interference under competitive conditions. The missing participant here, of course, is the buyer, who dismisses one seller in favor of the other one. Pettit gives no indication that this buyer arbitrarily interferes with the existing seller by dropping their services, nor does he imply that the good in question must be a product or service—it could be a factor of production, such as labor. If so, then an employer does not arbitrarily interfere with an employee by firing him in a competitive context; consequently, republican economic policy need not resort to empowering workers via voice (e.g., laws permitting closed-shop unions), except in cases where competitive conditions prove very difficult to establish and/or maintain.

Before concluding, I should address a potential concern about my reading of republican economic policy. Pettit says freedom as non-domination is an "inherently communitarian ideal," and as I noted in the introduction, Dagger emphasizes the need to "protect communities from the ravages of market competition," by which he means the instability and dislocation that can result from the mobility of labor and capital (Pettit 1997, 120; Dagger 2006, 163). Doesn't a one-sided focus on exit, especially for employees, threaten to produce a deracinated citizenry that lacks the durable relationships and other forms of social capital that are necessary to resist domination in other domains? One thing to keep in mind is that credible threats of exit will frequently not need to be exercised: employers, aware of the rich exit options of employees in a republican state, will anticipate exit and respond appropriately, by preemptively improving wages and other conditions of employment; to use the terminology of game theory, exit will be off the equilibrium path. For a variety of reasons, however—including the irrationality of one or both parties and asymmetric information—an exit-oriented republican economic policy will probably lead to greater, perhaps much greater, labor mobility. Whether the net effect of this rise will be to increase domination (as the objection implies) or decrease it (as I have maintained) depends upon a number of factors. For example, will a more mobile labor force merely shift their allegiances from local kinds of community to non-local kinds (e.g., national professional associations, political pressure groups, and online communities), and will these new kinds of community be just as effective at resisting domination? If not, might it still be the case that increased mobility will allow people to escape not only economic domination but also the domination caused by local communities themselves (whether domestic, ethnic, or religious), and might this dual reduction in domination outweigh the increased domination resulting from the putative erosion of localized social capital? (Pettit himself reminds us of the continuing vulnerability of women and minorities to domination by families and local majority communities—see Pettit 1997, 123–4, 138–40, 143–6.)

These are difficult questions to answer in the abstract, as they depend upon a complex set of sociological assessments, and republicans are likely to divide on this matter due to the burdens of judgment (Rawls 1993, 54–8). My own sense is that the above questions can be answered in the affirmative and that an exit-oriented republican economic policy is the best way of promoting freedom as non-domination. Moreover, as I have argued throughout the chapter, I believe that such a policy is generally consistent with the vision of republicanism presented by Pettit and does not depend upon a strained reading of his texts. Even Pettit's claim that freedom as non-domination is an "inherently communitarian ideal" is less about preserving local community and the social capital it embodies than about encouraging solidarity among those groups (such as women, racial minorities, immigrants, homosexuals, and the elderly) that are vulnerable to domination, and it is unclear why mobility would undermine such solidarity—it might even reinforce it if it weakened competing kinds of solidarity, including localism (Pettit 1997, 120–6). Having said this, however, I recognize that other republicans would be likely to answer the above questions in the negative and thus reject, in part or in whole, an exit-oriented economic policy; Dagger (2006, 163–4) and Michael Sandel (1996) would probably be among them. What this divergence indicates is simply the continuing diversity of the republican tradition, one that I noted earlier in this chapter and will discuss further in Chapters 4 and 5: it has both individualistic and communitarian strains, and they may generate somewhat divergent conclusions about economic policy. In view of the centrality of Pettit's theory to the neo-republican literature, however, this chapter's arguments should at least lead republicans of all stripes to reconsider if not revise their economic-policy positions.[8]

The Limits and Potential of Market Freedom

I have shown over the course of this chapter how economic competition restrains—and in the limit, eradicates—market power and how such restraint helps us to realize "market freedom," i.e., freedom as non-domination in the context of economic exchange. This finding means that a republican economic program should be primarily focused on promoting competitive conditions (including a plurality of informed buyers and sellers, free entry and exit, and price-taking rather than price-making behavior) and pursuing the policy

---

[8] Gourevitch (2013), echoing the claims of others (e.g., Krause 2013), has argued that Pettit's conception of freedom as non-domination "lacks an adequate conception of structural domination," viz., the domination of workers by their capitalist masters, and that nineteenth-century labor republicanism's more solidaristic conception of freedom entails labor's right to control the workplace (596, 609–10). As I argued above, though, the Anglo-Nordic package of policy instruments required by Pettit's neo-republicanism includes capitalist demogrants, which in combination with other, related policy tools (e.g., inheritance taxation) provides the means for democratizing ownership of private capital; by giving workers the option of exiting employment relationships and becoming capitalists if they choose to do so, such demogrants allow us to attack structural domination without having to wield the double-edged sword of voice. (See Taylor 2014, especially 453–4, for an elaboration of this argument in a non-republican context.)

innovations that would help us attain these conditions, such as informational campaigns, labor-market reform, aggressive antitrust, capitalist demogrants, and/or a basic income. These Anglo-Nordic reforms and the competitive conditions that they would support constitute an economic constitutionalism as important as the political constitutionalism with which republicans have traditionally been identified: perfect competition is a translation of the rule of law into the economic sphere.[9] Once republicans take this lesson to heart, they will (like their commercial-republican forefather Adam Smith) look upon competitive markets with enthusiasm, not mere "complacency" (Pettit 2006b, 142).

Republicans may worry, however, that perfect competition is a lofty ideal that real-world markets will rarely approach, much less attain, even if the republican economic program outlined above were fully implemented. This concern is a reasonable one, but it applies no less strongly to the other components of republicanism. The rule of law, the separation of powers, bicameralism, federalism, and international legalism are also demanding ideals that real-world political systems at best approximate rather than achieve, because political actors motivated by various sectional, economic, and ideological interests work persistently to sidestep and even undermine them. Both perfect competition and the rule of law are regulative ideals for republicans, ones that motivate and guide principled political action—and the closer we can approach them, the closer we will be to achieving non-domination in economic and political life.

This being said, we must always be alert to a problem first discussed in Chapter 1: non-monotonicity in the relationship between exit costs and the welfare of least-advantaged workers. If government does nothing but protect formal rights of movement and occupational choice, then abusive employers will prompt an exodus of their most advantaged employees, diminishing the voices of those they leave behind and perhaps realizing Hirschman's worst fears. To prevent this eventuality, governments must transform partial-exit worlds into free-exit ones by making use of the full panoply of Anglo-Nordic economic policies; they must not only promote competition in labor markets but also resource exit through various government services and income transfers. Relatedly, we should be aware that these policies are not à la carte: they must be implemented in tandem, because pursuing merely a subset of them may increase rather than decrease domination. For instance, a sharp attack on union privilege without similar efforts to limit employer collusion in particular labor markets (e.g., hospital nursing and dental hygiene) and enhance labor mobility may just

---

[9] As Michel Foucault notes, the German Ordoliberals similarly demanded "the application to the economy of what is called *Rechtsstaat* in the German tradition..." (2008, 167–8).

make workers more vulnerable to the market power of capitalists, a point Smith himself made long ago (Smith 1981, 83–5 [I.viii.11–14]). We must always bear in mind that deregulation and liberalization can be spurred as much by rent-seeking behavior as regulation and protection. This fact is not an argument for maintaining anti-competitive practices but rather a reminder that as we approach these tasks we ought to keep a wary eye on what Jeremy Bentham referred to as "sinister interests."

Even if this Anglo-Nordic policy package were implemented in full, though, it would not entirely solve the problem of market domination due to both natural and legal limits on economic agency. Market freedom presumes such agency; workers without it would lack the ability to hold their employers accountable and defend their own interests through voice or exit. In some cases, however, it will either be absent (e.g., the severely mentally disabled) or present only in a limited way (e.g., many of the elderly); exit will have to be supplanted by voice here, be it in the form of the regulation option or perhaps the participation option. Far less extreme forms of compromised psychological agency are imaginable and may also justify regulatory interventions. To cite Smith again, he worried that a minute division of labor, though efficient, might be mentally deadening for laborers:

> The man whose whole life is spent in performing a few simple operations, of which the effects too are, perhaps, always the same, or very nearly the same, has no occasion to exert his understanding, or to exercise his invention in finding out expedients for removing difficulties which never occur. He naturally loses, therefore, the habit of such exertion, and generally becomes as stupid and ignorant as it is possible for a human creature to become.... But in every improved and civilized society this is the state into which the labouring poor, that is, the great body of the people, must necessarily fall, unless government takes some pains to prevent it. (Smith 1981, 781–2 [V.i.f.50]; cf. Mill 1991, 254–5 ["drive a quill"])

If workers' psychological agency is hobbled by such production methods, they may be less likely to take advantage of policies that resource exit and more likely to require regulatory assistance, be it in the shape of working-time directives or compulsory, state-subsidized education for their children, as Smith himself suggests (1981, 785–8 [V.i.f.54–61]).

More disturbingly, there are often legal limits on economic agency that may call for voice as a second-best corrective. Consider the case of California farmworkers who are in the country illegally. It would be difficult to resource their exit from abusive employment relations because deportation fears would make them hesitant to apply for such state support in the first place; also, because a small group of families has often owned farmland in certain areas for a long period of time, collusion is not only likely but also hard to police due to codes of silence

(Daniel 1981). As a result, the privatization option of the United Farm Workers union, while far from perfect, might be better than no action at all. A far better solution, of course, would be to legalize these workers, aggressively pursue antitrust action against the colluding farm employers, resource exit via travel and relocation vouchers, and so forth, but these actions may simply be politically infeasible. We therefore have to remain open to the direct empowerment of voice *in extremis*, despite its many serious drawbacks.

In closing, I'd like to point out that my friendly amendment to neo-republicanism, which I believe to be consistent with not only its spirit but its letter, helps bring it into tighter alignment with various other approaches to political economy. Economists promote perfect competition for the sake of welfare, libertarians and liberals for the sake of autonomy and (expanded) choice, and republicans (so I have argued) for the sake of non-domination. Each shares a commitment to the same mediating institution but sees different ultimate values at stake in its achievement. Such an overlapping consensus clearly strengthens the case for competitive markets, but it also helps neo-republicanism appear more modern and moderate and therefore more attractive to adherents of competitor doctrines. If republicanism retains the whiff of austere anti-commercialism thanks to earlier republicans like Rousseau, then nothing will better dispel it than a wider realization that true republicanism celebrates competitive markets.

4

State

Republicans have long been focused on the problem of arbitrary political power and have explored a variety of solutions, most notably constitutional ones that safeguard citizens by means of the dispersal of political power, such as the checks and balances associated with the separation of powers, bicameralism, international legalism, and especially federalism (Pettit 1997, 177–80). Earlier republican supporters of federalism, including Montesquieu, Rousseau, and Kant, viewed confederal interstate arrangements as a way to combine the virtues of small republics with those of large monarchies (viz., political non-domination and military power, respectively) and secure international peace (Montesquieu 1989, 131–3; Rousseau 2005, 53–60; Kant 1996, 311–51).[1] The authors of *The Federalist Papers* developed these ideas further, applying them to an interlocking federal arrangement among the American states. Hamilton, quoting Montesquieu in *Federalist 9*, emphasized the way that dividing sovereignty between the states and federal government would protect citizens from domination by the authorities at either level; Madison echoes this thought in *Federalist 51*: "the different governments will control each other, at the same time that each will be controlled by itself" (Publius 2003, 35–40, 251–5).

Contemporary republicans, on the other hand, have had little to say regarding federalism, and what they have had to say has been surprisingly flat and unrevealing (e.g., Pettit 1997, 178–9; Bohman 2009, 60, 73). This reticence is in striking contrast with the contemporary revival of federalism among liberal multiculturalists, who see in it a solution to the problem of "how rival minority and majority nationalist projects can be accommodated within the democratic structures of a single (federal) state" (Norman 2006, vii; also see Norman 1994, Kymlicka 2001, Weinstock 2001, de Schutter 2011). One of the contributors to this literature, Iris Marion Young, even steals a march on republicans by

---

[1] I set to one side the heated debate over Montesquieu's republican credentials; for some contributions to this debate, see Pangle (1973), Rahe (2009), Douglass (2012), and de Dijn (2014). Pettit, for one, labels him a republican (1997, 19; 2012, 7).

defending her unusual form of "horizontal federalism" (which aims to protect both minority groups and minorities within minorities) on the republican ground of non-domination—and this despite her criticisms of republicanism elsewhere (Young 2005; cf. Young 1989).

Contemporary republicans (and liberal multiculturalists, for that matter) have failed to see that federalism, in addition to providing participatory and constitutional checks on the exercise of arbitrary political power, offers a more market-oriented approach as well, an economic model of political republicanism that harnesses both competitive markets and resourced exit in the service of non-domination.[2] In this model, a mobile citizenry places political sub-units—cities, counties, and provinces—into vigorous competition with each other for residents and businesses; far from a race to the bottom, this competition can, if properly regulated and resourced, constrain arbitrary power and force sub-units to track citizen preferences. In the limit, such competition can not only complement but even to some degree substitute for political voice, lessening our reliance on the vagaries of democratic control and providing an alternative path to realizing Pettit's desiderata of individualization, unconditionality, and efficacy, as we shall soon discover (Pettit 2012, 166–79). This economic model of political republicanism can never entirely displace the participatory and constitutional approaches, of course, especially as we ascend the hierarchy of political sub-units and exit becomes increasingly costly in ways that cannot be finessed by constitutional, legal, and policy reforms. Still, even if exit cannot substitute for voice in the political realm to the degree that it can in the domestic and economic realms, I shall argue in this chapter that its potential role in promoting political freedom has been underappreciated, especially by neo-republicans.

I start, as I have in the previous two chapters, by contrasting political power and political freedom, with the former understood here as a condition of political domination and exploitation made possible by the absence of democratic control, constitutional checks and balances, and/or a meaningful exit option, and the latter understood as the limitation and even negation of this kind of power. Holding fixed participatory and constitutional remedies to such power, which are types of voice, I explore the alternative, economic remedy that I sketched above, which relies upon exit instead, here in the form of citizen mobility. As I'll show, the success of this alternative approach depends upon not only formal freedom of movement across political sub-units but also efforts to augment competition between these sub-units by means of both subsidiarity

---

[2] Spitz (2009, 296) is a partial exception to this claim, to which I shall return below.

and fiscal federalism and resource exit through policy reforms as varied as health-insurance portability and relocation vouchers. In the next section, I demonstrate that this market model of political freedom is a kind of antipower on Pettit's own understanding of the term: first, because it limits the ability of local political leaders to interfere with impunity and at will in the interests of their local residents and businesses and even forces them to promote these interests; second, because it realizes the equal popular control Pettit prizes, characterized by individualization, unconditionality, and efficacy. I also respond in this section to Pettit's own doubts about exit's potential as a form of antipower in political contexts and, more generally, to his concern that such reliance upon market mechanisms in politics might objectionably "background reason" (Pettit 1997, 203); I confront too the worries of communitarian republicans like Richard Dagger, who think that high levels of citizen mobility may undermine the conditions of republican self-government (Dagger 1997, 154–72). Finally, in the conclusion I emphasize that a successful defense of political freedom requires an optimal mix of participatory, constitutional, and economic means, one that will vary across time and levels of government but will rarely be all voice or exit, and moreover that the very implementation of an economic model of political republicanism will demand participatory and constitutional means.

Before beginning, however, I would like to pause to say a few words about my use of the term "political freedom." This term has tremendous historical resonance, yet my use of it might seem idiosyncratic, perhaps even deliberately misleading, so it is not enough for me to say that I am just using it as a term of art. In both everyday and academic use, political freedom (or liberty) is generally understood to mean what it means to Rawls: the rights to vote and hold public office, i.e., rights to democratic political participation (Rawls 1993, 4–7, 284, 327–31, 417). This voice-oriented understanding of political freedom, however common, is not the only one available, and in the republican political tradition it has taken on a wider meaning: freedom as non-domination (Pettit 1997, 25; Lovett and Pettit 2009, 13). Democratic political participation is certainly one way to advance political freedom so defined, but then so are constitutional means, including ones that *restrain* the voice of the people, such as written bills of rights, judicial review, etc. Thus, my use of political freedom in this chapter, which widens it even further so as to include market-like mechanisms that reduce domination by forcing political sub-units to compete for mobile citizens, is consistent with the spirit if not the letter of contemporary republican usage, even as it deviates to some degree from common usage.

Political Power versus Political Freedom

In Chapter 3, I suggested that labor monopsony is market power in its most extreme and disturbing form. The totalitarian state is its analogue with respect to political power. Such a state, in its "ideal" form, superintends a completely closed society lacking any democratic participation or institutional checks and balances on its one-man or one-party rule. North Korea is the closest contemporary approach to this ideal: Kim Jong-un's control over his subjects is exactly the kind of power Pettit has in mind when he says that a capacity to interfere with impunity and at will, when it is "fully realized," "amounts to an absolutely arbitrary power" (Pettit 1996, 580; Demick 2010). For our purposes, though, the German Democratic Republic (i.e., the former East German communist state) will offer a more illuminating, albeit historical, example.

The GDR was ruled de facto by the Politburo of the Socialist Unity Party; this one-party (or one-committee) rule morphed into one-man rule under Erich Honecker, general secretary of the Politburo from 1971 until 1989. Party leaders monopolized all significant state posts, keeping the state apparatus under the control of the Party and eliminating any possible internal checks on its power. Some external checks existed—Honecker craved international respect, depended upon West German transfers to keep his bankrupt state afloat, and took marching orders from Moscow on important matters due to the continuing presence of Soviet troops in the country—but these either did little to reduce Party domination of East German citizens or, in the case of the Soviets, actually reinforced it. The Ministry for State Security, known as the Stasi, was the instrument of this domination, running a system of surveillance and terror that destroyed trust among citizens, including families; over the lifetime of the regime, 250,000 people served as full-time Stasi staff while another 600,000 served as informants—and this in a country of only 17 million. This cruel, pervasive system of arbitrary power facilitated forms of exploitation more commonly associated with criminal gangs than states. For example, the Party allowed the West German government to purchase the freedom of separated family members, political prisoners, and others (about 33,000 from 1963 to 1989) according to an established schedule of prices euphemistically called "transit sums": 4,500 Deutschmarks for a separated family member, 96,000 for a political prisoner, etc. (Sarotte 2014, 6–14). The East German state quite literally took its own citizens hostage.

Unsurprisingly, one of the Stasi's primary jobs was border control, as no comprehensive system of state terror can long survive if people are free to exit it. The West German state offered East Germans who could reach its soil an immediate right to a passport and social services, and the Party therefore realized relatively early that limiting citizen mobility would be a *sine qua non* of its continued power. The construction of the Berlin Wall starting in 1961 was prompted by the flight of large numbers of working-age citizens; these efforts were extended to other parts of the border, where electrified fences, armed guards, attack dogs, and even antipersonnel mines were used to deter potential "deserters." Numerous factors played a role in the eventual collapse of the East German regime, including Gorbachev's reform agenda and the protests in Leipzig, Dresden, and East Berlin in 1989, but the exodus that followed Hungary's decision to allow East Germans to transit through their country to Austria and the unintended opening of the Berlin Wall a mere two months later were crucial, as they sharply intensified pressure on a weakened regime (ibid.). Voice and exit worked in tandem here to undermine a totalitarian dictatorship, with exit not only draining the state of workers (and potential hostages) but also amplifying the voices of those who remained behind: only accession to citizens' demands for civil liberties and free elections would stanch the flow of East Germans to the West.

This example illustrates how mobility can be a threat to those holding political power and can potentially serve as a tool for those pursuing political freedom. Totalitarian and authoritarian regimes have long recognized this fact, imposing restrictions on not just emigration but internal movement as well. China's household-registration (*hukou*) system is a case in point: by limiting the ability of rural residents to migrate to coastal cities, it disperses dissent and thereby enhances the stability of Communist rule (Wallace 2014, ch. 6). Conversely, enabling mobility should limit political power, both by allowing the oppressed to escape its influence and by making their threats to exit unless they are accommodated more credible to their oppressors. If mobility could be made frictionless and political sub-units could be incentivized to compete with each other for residents in the same way that firms in a perfectly competitive market compete with one another for customers, political power at the local level, at least, could be extinguished. Granted, such a scenario is an ideal type that can be approached but never fully attained in practice; moreover, as we shall see, its very operation is dependent upon participatory and constitutional supports, so it could never be a comprehensive substitute for political voice. Nevertheless, this economic model of political republicanism can serve as a regulative ideal, one that guides policymaking and helps lessen our reliance on readily corruptible democratic mechanisms of control.

The canonical statement of this model—which was made in an intellectual context utterly unconnected with academic political philosophy, much less republicanism—is Charles Tiebout's seminal "A Pure Theory of Local Expenditures" (Tiebout 1956). This article, a response to Paul Samuelson's even more influential "A Pure Theory of Public Expenditure" (Samuelson 1954), is an attempt to prove that, contra Samuelson, there is a decentralized, competitive solution to the free-rider problem in public-goods provision for a certain class of public goods, viz., local public goods, such as "police and fire protection, education, hospitals, and courts" (Tiebout 1956, 418). Tiebout envisions a continuum of local communities offering different mixes of public goods at different prices (i.e., tax rates), which fully mobile and fully informed "consumer-voters" choose among, picking the communities that best satisfy their preferences for public goods. Competition between these communities for residents drives them to produce their particular mix of goods at the lowest possible cost; threat of entry by new communities also disciplines the pricing behavior of existing communities, even those with an apparent monopoly on their public-goods blend.[3] A variety of other assumptions round out the model: there are no negative or positive "spillovers" across communities (e.g., pollution and pest control, respectively); due to the presence of a fixed factor, such as land, there exist optimal community sizes at which average costs are minimized; communities try to attain their optimal size through various policies, such as tax breaks for new residents and zoning restrictions to limit growth; and so forth (Tiebout 1956, 419–20).

One relatively undertheorized aspect of Tiebout's model is the production side: how and why do communities produce the particular mix of public goods that they do? Here is what little he has to say about the matter:

> On the production side it is assumed that communities are forced to keep production costs at a minimum either through the efficiency of city managers or through competition from other communities.... In this model and in reality, the city manager or elected official who is not able to keep his costs (taxes) low compared with those of similar communities will find himself out of a job. (Tiebout 1956, 422)

His comments here are consistent with at least a couple of understandings of how production and budgetary decisions are made: what Wallace Oates refers to as the "entrepreneurial version" and the "collective-choice version" (Oates 2006, 29–32). The first, which relies entirely on the power of exit and is consequently most in the spirit of Tiebout's overall model, treats communities as private developments started by profit-seeking entrepreneurs who employ managers to run them. This version turns "consumer-voters" into consumer-movers who vote solely with their feet, just as consumers in normal markets use choice instead of voice to pick the kind of product or service they want; democracy is dispensed

---

[3] That is, these communities operate in a "contestable market," characterized by an absence of entry/exit barriers and sunk costs and by universal access to public-goods production technologies (Baumol et al. 1982).

with entirely, at least internal to the communities themselves. (See, for example, Sonstelie and Portney 1978 and Henderson 1985.) The second version, on the other hand, assumes that residents in these communities will be able to vote at the ballot box as well as with their feet, correcting city managers with both voice and exit. But as William Fischel has pointed out:

> Tiebout's neglect of local government politics requires only modest amendment of his model. In most local governments one just has to replace Tiebout's invisible municipal managers with the median-voter model. *The median voter will want to do most of the same things that an entrepreneurial private manager would want to do.* (Fischel 2001, 96; emphasis added)

If this is true, however, then political voice will add little to the entrepreneurial model: we could do away with democratic participation at the local level and end up with a very similar outcome, but one without the various risks of politics (e.g., interest-group "capture" of city managers). In other words, just as workers have no need for industrial democracy so long as labor markets are perfectly competitive and exit is resourced, so consumer-movers have no need for local political democracy so long as the locational market is perfectly competitive and mobility is frictionless.[4]

To see how this economic model advances republicanism's objective of non-domination, consider the case of a denizen of some community on the continuum who is exposed to arbitrary power exercised by the city manager or some other functionary. Because mobility is frictionless and communities offering the same or similar mix of public goods *without* such arbitrary power either exist or could freely enter, this denizen and others in the same situation could either exit or credibly threaten to do so; the dominating community would therefore have to cease to dominate or, if it refused, lose its population to other communities. Community officials who try to exploit their residents (e.g., by demanding bribes or charging extortionate fees for standard services) will suffer the same fate: perfect competition between communities combined with a mobile citizenry will tend to drain exploitative jurisdictions of residents (Epple and Zelenitz 1981). Finally, return to the example with which I started this volume: stop-and-frisks by police engaged in illicit racial profiling. Under the hypothesized conditions, such discriminatory actions would also lead to an exodus of residents, this time

---

[4] As Pettit reminds us in a different context, "the second element [voice] is not strictly necessary for the absence of domination. Even if the exercise of the power—the interference practiced—were not otherwise under the control of the interferees, the fact that they could set aside the arrangement at will [e.g., by migrating] would make for a certain sort of control; it would give them the power of exit" (2014, 221n62).

racial minorities and those non-minorities outraged by racist cops and complicit officials. Tiebout's pure theory of local expenditures, just like the theory of perfect competition in product and factor markets, is therefore properly described as an economic model of (political) republicanism.[5]

None of this is to say, of course, that community officials in the Tiebout model will lack discretionary power. As I pointed out in the previous chapter, administrative efficiency will often require that government agents be permitted "a substantial degree of discretion," lest we forego "all possibility of fitting government action to the needs of particular cases" (Pettit 1997, 175–6). Discretionary power need not be arbitrary power, however. The Tiebout model puts citizens in a position to pick from a continuum of communities differing by kind and degree of administrative discretion exercised inter alia. Such choice guarantees that this residual administrative discretion is non-arbitrary, as it "tracks the interests…of the person suffering the interference" (Pettit 1997, 55). These choices will typically involve tradeoffs (e.g., less discretion may mean higher taxes or a lower quality of service), but so long as the market in communities is perfectly competitive and mobility is frictionless, such tradeoffs can reasonably be viewed as tracking citizen interests.

Given the Tiebout model's radical and at times unrealistic assumptions (e.g., the absence of spillovers between communities and the existence of fully informed/mobile citizen-movers), it may appear distressingly unrelated to the world that we actually inhabit. As decades of empirical studies have shown, though, jurisdictional competition does in fact operate in much the way that the Tiebout model describes. For example, an early article by Oates (1969) noticed an important implication of Tiebout's model: if mobile households really do shop for local public goods at the lowest possible price, then the differential between local public outputs and local taxes should be reflected in local property values. Oates tested for this "capitalization" by using a sample of New Jersey local governments and discovered that increased spending on public schools paid for with local taxes led to higher property values, precisely as he predicted. Literally dozens of follow-up studies on capitalization have confirmed Oates' original conjecture (Fischel 2001, 39–71). Such shopping around by consumer-movers

---

[5] Though Tiebout does not directly address issues of domination, exploitation, and discrimination, he does point out that "non-economic variables will also be considered" by citizen-voters in picking their home, and these three issues would surely play a role in that choice (Tiebout 1956, 418). Moreover, one might convert these non-economic issues into economic ones by seeing them as just an informal price or tax imposed on residents by dominating, exploitative, and/or discriminatory communities. In either case, though, my attempt to appropriate Tiebout's theory for republican purposes is consistent with the spirit of his theory and even, I believe, its letter.

should also force local governments to be more efficient, and there is a substantial literature confirming this Tiebout hypothesis as well. Hoxby (2000), for instance, finds that local public-school competition (as measured by the number of public-school districts in a student's metropolitan statistical area) has a significant positive effect on test scores. Robert Inman sums up the numerous empirical tests of the Tiebout model as follows:

> Though piecemeal, the econometric evidence is uniformly supportive of the Tiebout conjecture. Households demand local public goods in a manner consistent with utility maximization. Local governments supply local public goods in a manner consistent with cost minimization. Local fiscal competition within large metropolitan areas control local government costs and appears to provide sufficient choice to households to ensure overall allocative efficiency. (Inman 2006, 52)

These studies might leave the false impression that jurisdictional competition and citizen mobility are important primarily for their ability to deliver good public educations to the children of well-heeled homeowners, but they are even more important for the benefits they deliver to the most vulnerable members of our nation. Historical examples abound of disadvantaged minorities who have fled domination, exploitation, and discrimination in one part of the country for a better life in another, in the process generating pressure for change both in their new homes and in the places they left behind. The most famous of these were the various phases of the Great Migration of African Americans out of the South during the Jim Crow era (Wilkerson 2010). This exodus to the North, West, and more tolerant parts of the South not only enriched the cultures of these regions and catalyzed political change there but also forced especially intolerant Southern cities and states to modify their oppressive policies (e.g., by cracking down on lynching and improving property protections and educational opportunities) so as to retain their cheap supply of domestic and agricultural labor (Somin 2010, 218). A similar, if less dramatic, process can be observed in the internal migration of gays and lesbians to more tolerant cities and states (Clark 2003).

What these examples indicate, however, is not just the promise of Tiebout sorting and the interjurisdictional competition it induces but also their limits, at least under historical conditions. The ongoing liberation of African Americans, gays, and lesbians from various forms of localized oppression, although certainly helped by foot voting, has mostly been driven by participatory and constitutional means (e.g., the various referenda, legislative votes, and court decisions to legalize gay marriage, usually over local objections). These apparent limits of the Tiebout model are due not to intrinsic problems with it but rather to a failure to secure its preconditions: viz., resourced exit and robust competition. The right to exit local jurisdictions remains formal, not substantive, and interjurisdictional competition has been suppressed by various characteristics of federal and state constitutions, laws, and policies. The tragic consequences of the failure to resource exit can be seen most clearly in the historical "black flight" example from Chapter 1 and the related but contemporary controversy about police abuse in minority communities, ranging from the kind of profiling discussed above to racially-motivated assault and even murder. The African Americans who remain trapped in these dysfunctional inner-city communities lack the resources to move on and, even if they had them, may be misinformed about opportunities elsewhere, whether in terms of superior policing and other local services (such as schools) or better job markets. In order for jurisdictional competition to play a constructive role in the lives of our least-advantaged citizens, more will have to be done to enable their exit from abusive—or simply neglectful—communities and to cause the leaders of these communities to anticipate the fiscal and economic pain of their departure.

Consider first the issue of mobility. Interstate freedom of movement has been recognized as a fundamental constitutional right at least since *Corfield v. Coryell* (1823), which was an early circuit-court decision, but the US Supreme Court case *Saenz v. Roe* (1999), which relies upon the Constitution's "privileges and immunities" clause and its Fourteenth Amendment citizenship clause, rendered it official.[6] This constitutional entrenchment of the right to enter and exit local jurisdictions is merely a formal protection, however, not a substantive one: ignorance or poverty may seriously undermine one's willingness or ability to exercise this right. Certain actions by the federal government, like its interstate transportation-infrastructure investments, may have helped the least advantaged exercise it, but on the whole moving has remained a do-it-yourself project, one that the educated and the affluent have historically found easier to accomplish.

In this context, it is important to note that mobility rates in the United States have been falling since the mid-1960s, from about 20 percent of the population switching residences each year to a little over 11 percent today (Ihrke 2014, 1). There has been ample speculation about the fundamental causes of this secular trend, especially demographic ones (e.g., an aging population and increase in the number of two-earner households, both of which should depress mobility), though other, less noticed changes to the economy might be the true culprits, including increasing homogeneity in labor markets and better, more readily available information about those markets (Kaplan and Schulhofer-Wohl 2013). For our purposes, though, what is most disturbing about these mobility

---

[6] Similar protection for the liberties of movement and residence was effectively provided by Article 12 of the Treaty of Rome (European Union 1957), which established the European Economic Community.

statistics are the differences across socioeconomic groups. Consider just two striking examples: about half of college graduates leave their birth states by age thirty, but only 27 percent of high-school graduates and 17 percent of high-school dropouts do (Moretti 2012, 157); among intercounty movers in 2013, those earning under $30,000 per year were about 30 percent less likely to make a "national" move (over 500 miles) as those over $30,000 per year (US Census Bureau 2013). This relative lack of both interstate and interregional mobility among the less educated and poor can be traced in large part to financial factors, such as the expense of a long move and the need to remain close to a network of family and friends who can be relied upon for support in hard times, but also to difficulties in accessing and evaluating information about work opportunities, housing costs, and the quality of public services in distant cities.

Such immobility is costly. At the Great Recession's peak, for example, unemployment in Detroit reached 20 percent, but just 500 miles to the west in Iowa City it was a mere 4 percent (Moretti 2012, 157). The ability to move in search of work can yield large dividends in the face of this degree of variation in unemployment rates. Moreover, as Enrico Moretti has argued in his recent book *The New Geography of Jobs*, job creation—both skilled and unskilled—is highly concentrated in a handful of national "innovation hubs," including places like the San Francisco Bay Area, Austin, Raleigh-Durham, Boston-Cambridge, San Diego, New York City, Washington (DC), Seattle, and Portland (Moretti 2012, especially chs 2 and 3). Getting to these areas is essential—and not just for work: they are also characterized by better health and longevity, lower rates of divorce, higher rates of political participation and charitable giving, and greater intergenerational income mobility, with the last driven in part by higher-quality public education (Moretti 2012, 107–20; Chetty et al. 2014, Chetty et al. 2015, Chetty and Hendren 2015).

Increasing mobility rates for the least advantaged is a daunting task, one that will have to proceed along a variety of different policy dimensions. One of the most important dimensions is informational: getting high-quality, easy-to-digest data about employment opportunities, housing costs, and school quality in different metropolitan areas into the hands of the poor. Although the various government statistical bureaus will have to play a central role in this, such an effort will be for naught unless the poor can access the place where such information is most easily posted: the Internet. The so-called "digital divide" places the poor at a great disadvantage in access to the Internet: only 40 percent of those earning under $30,000 per year have broadband at home, compared to 87 percent of those earning over $75,000 per year (Jansen 2010). Bridging this divide might be done directly, through home-broadband subsidies, or indirectly, by improving Internet access at public libraries.

Even if the poor were fully informed about such opportunities, though, various obstacles to moving remain in their way. One that has been mostly removed by the Affordable Care Act is the absence of health-insurance portability. Another is the risk of losing various kinds of welfare support: unless these are portable too, the poor will be resistant to moving, especially when such moves will take them far away from the support networks of friends and family. Welfare reforms that gave the states greater discretion in designing programs, determining eligibility, etc., have been fruitful in many ways, but the federal government still has a key role to play in coordinating these efforts so that mobility among recipients is not discouraged, perhaps by assuring a decent social minimum that is invariant across states (Spitz 2009, 296). Another obstacle that will occur to anyone who is familiar with the innovation hubs listed above is housing costs: these are very desirable locations and have correspondingly pricey rental markets. Rental vouchers for the poor are one way of dealing with this problem, but so are efforts to increase the supply of affordable housing in these places, whether by modifying zoning laws to allow denser growth or improving public transit so the poor can commute more easily (Moretti 2012, 176–7; *The Economist* 2016).

The most direct and radical approach to improving the mobility of the poor—but also the most promising, I think—is relocation vouchers that cover some or all of the costs of an intercity move, including moving expenses proper (moving van, air flights, etc.), security deposits on new apartments, and so on. The federal Trade Adjustment Assistance program, which helps workers who have lost their jobs to foreign trade, already offers relocation assistance; such aid could and should be extended to the entire pool of disadvantaged workers (Moretti 2012, 163). The results of an experiment run in the 1990s suggest that relocation vouchers could offer significant benefits for the uneducated and the poor. In the Move to Opportunity (MTO) program, randomly-selected residents of public housing in Baltimore, Boston, Chicago, Los Angeles, and New York were offered mobility counseling and a housing voucher to move to a different, less impoverished part of the city. Five years later, the experimental group had made substantial improvements over the control group in terms of both obesity reduction and mental health (distress, depression, anxiety, sleep, and calmness); unfortunately, adult economic self-sufficiency (earnings, welfare support) was unaffected (Kling et al. 2007). One reason for this last result, however, is relatively easy to discern: MTO only enabled moves *within* cities, but as Moretti remarks, "today it is differences *across* cities that are more likely to be the source of mismatch [between where the poor live and where the jobs are]" (Moretti 2012, 163–4;

cf. Chetty et al. 2015; Wilson 1987). So my proposed relocation voucher might best be restricted to intercity moves, as I originally suggested, in order to encourage resettlement in places with better job prospects, public services, etc.

As we have seen, increasing mobility among our least-advantaged citizens is a promising way to reduce their vulnerability to arbitrary power and improve their welfare. Cities vary widely in the quality of their public services (especially their schools and policing) and job markets, so converting the poor's merely formal right of geographic exit to a substantive one offers them the same kinds of opportunities the more affluent have to restart their lives in richer, safer, and more progressive places. But this only deals with the demand side of the problem, so to speak. In order for our economic model of political republicanism to reach its full potential, we must also make sure that cities face the proper incentives to supply the most attractive mixes of public services at the lowest possible prices (i.e., tax rates). In other words, we must do everything in our power to intensify jurisdictional competition for a newly mobile citizenry; we can then reasonably hope to approach if not reach the ideal of a perfectly competitive locational marketplace, one that purges power from the political system and thereby establishes full political freedom, at least at the local level.

How might this interjurisdictional struggle be amplified? The most effective way to do so is with *subsidiarity*, i.e., "the principle that a central authority should have a subsidiary function, performing only those tasks which cannot be performed effectively at a more immediate or local level" (OED Online 2015). The form of subsidiarity that is most relevant in our context is *fiscal federalism*, which decentralizes tax-and-spending decisions for local public goods to the relevant level of government (city, county, state, etc.), leaving the federal government to handle spillover effects across jurisdictions (by means of policy coordination, compensatory taxes and subsidies, etc.), deliver truly national public goods (e.g., national defense), ensure macroeconomic stability, and engage in income redistribution (Oates 1999, 1121–2). As Oates explains, doing so will best promote social welfare:

> By tailoring the outputs of [local public] goods and services to the particular preferences and circumstances of their constituencies, decentralized provision increases economic welfare above that which results from the more uniform levels of such services that are likely under national provision. The basic point here is simply that the efficient level of output of a local public good...is likely to vary across jurisdictions as a result of both differences in preferences and cost differentials. (Ibid.)[7]

---

[7] Oates (1972, 35, 54–63) provides a "Decentralization Theorem" that enumerates the sufficient conditions for fiscal federalism to be welfare-enhancing.

Because Tiebout sorting will make jurisdictions more homogeneous in terms of demand for local public goods, it will tend to increase the welfare gains of fiscal decentralization (Oates 2006, 40). For our purposes, though, the greatest advantage of fiscal federalism is its effect of putting every fiscal tub on its own bottom, i.e., forcing every local jurisdiction to pay for its own public goods. As a consequence of this, local government will have a robust incentive to attract and keep both residents and businesses, lest its tax base vanish and its public-goods mix become unaffordable. This induced competition for a mobile citizenry will constrain the ability of local governments to exploit, dominate, and discriminate against their residents—even, in the limit, wholly eliminating it. Fiscal federalism, by offering supply-side incentives to complement our demand-side mobility resourcing, completes the economic model of political republicanism.[8]

Throwing every jurisdiction on its own resources may appear unfair, given that some are likely to be poorer than others. The solution to this problem, however, is not redistribution from one jurisdiction to another, much less a return to fiscal centralism, but rather redistribution from rich to poor *individuals* on a *national* basis. As I remarked above, fiscal federalism assumes that income redistribution will have to be organized at the federal level: otherwise, local governments that engage in substantial redistribution will attract poor residents and cause richer ones to flee, leading to fiscal insolvency.[9] That such "social dumping" might occur is no argument for overall fiscal centralization, though: as Robert Inman wryly points out, "to combat hunger, we subsidize the poor's purchase of food; we do not shut down the marketplace and centralize food production and allocation" (Inman 2006, 53). In fact, general fiscal centralization tends to create a version of the so-called "resource curse" (Auty 1993): local governments, as dependents of the central state that finances them, have no incentive to attend to the needs of their own residents and businesses because foot voting has no effect on their bottom line—unless the central state attempts to mimic the pressure of foot voting in the Tiebout model by linking fiscal disbursements to population or business counts.

---

[8] So far, I have assumed that geographic exit is done by individuals or households, but we could also imagine entire jurisdictions exiting, i.e., secession. Entrenching such a collective exit right might help geographically-concentrated minorities resist domination by leaving or threatening to do so. See Weinstock (2001, 80–1) for further discussion.

[9] Note that federal organization of redistribution is not necessarily inconsistent with a certain degree of local or state discretion in carrying out federal mandates: the informational advantages of such discretion (e.g., allowing a degree of experimentation and learning that, if successful, can be observed and copied by others) might compensate for any disadvantages, such as somewhat unequal support for the poor across jurisdictions. This was presumably part of the justification for certain Clinton-era welfare reforms.

This last example raises the question of what residual role participatory and constitutional checks may have in our proposed economic model, especially at the local level. Quoting Fischel, I noted earlier that if "entrepreneurial private managers" of cities want to do much the same thing as the median voter, then the entrepreneurial and collective-choice versions of the Tiebout model will generate similar results, rendering local democracy superfluous or even contraindicated. The success of this claim depends upon the assumptions of the Tiebout model being met, though, and there are reasons to believe that they will not be met and that the ideal of a perfectly competitive locational marketplace will be harder to approximate than I have implied so far. On the demand side, frictionless mobility will be difficult to approach, much less achieve, even with the kind of resourcing that I suggested above: quitting your job, selling your house, and leaving your family and friends behind to relocate to a distant city is likely to have major professional, financial, and psychic costs that will discourage many, especially the risk averse. On the supply side, difficulty in establishing new jurisdictions or changing the operation of existing ones will limit competitive pressure on incumbents, creating enough space for arbitrary power to creep back into the system. The analogy I have been relying on throughout this chapter—namely, that locational competition between jurisdictions for a mobile citizenry is like the competition between businesses in product and factor markets for customers—is problematic, because it is considerably easier to stop using one business in favor of its nearby competitor than it is to move to another city with better public services than your own, and it is much simpler to open a new business to compete with cossetted incumbents than it is to start a new city or take over an old one. Political freedom cannot simply be reduced to market freedom.

Consequently, participatory and constitutional checks will be required to complement the kind of pressure that resourced exit and enhanced competition can bring to bear on local political leaders, whether in the form of local elections or federal supervision and regulation of these local authorities. More generally, what we must do in order to minimize political domination is find an optimal mix of accountability mechanisms, one that will vary by level in the hierarchy of federal institutions. Such variation should follow a predictable pattern: the lower we go in the hierarchy, the more we will be able to rely upon exit and the less we will have to rely upon voice—though we will never be able to dispense with voice, despite its challenges. As I have argued throughout the chapter, the closer we get to the level of the city or neighborhood, the easier it is to move and the more nearby options we have for moving; this increases competitive pressures, especially if mobility is properly resourced and fiscal federalism is in place. Conversely, the closer we get to the level of the state or nation, the harder it is to move and the fewer options we have for moving away; consequently, competitive pressures are weak, and participatory and constitutional checks will become increasingly important, even dominant. At the national level, in fact, the economic model of political republicanism loses most its force as an accountability mechanism: emigration is just too difficult and expensive to serve as an effective check—except for wealthy individuals and multinationals—and this fundamental limitation cannot be finessed with mobility vouchers and the like, at least at this time. Note, moreover, that only this federal framework can make our economic model an effective accountability mechanism at the lower levels of the hierarchy, that only it can offer the various resources for intercity and interstate mobility and provide state and local governments with the proper incentives to compete. Political voice at the national level, in other words, turns out to be a crucial condition for successful political exit at the state and local level—a point to which I shall return in the chapter's conclusion.[10]

Political Freedom as Antipower

For a moment, however, I want to set to one side these limitations of the economic model in order to explore more thoroughly its capacity for curbing arbitrary power. The political model, after all, has monopolized attention in the republican literature until now, with Pettit's two major republican texts relying very heavily on it. As a consequence, I do not believe we are sufficiently cognizant—or even conscious at all—of the economic model's advantages vis-à-vis the political model. For this reason, I will continue for now to discuss

---

[10] My Tiebout-inspired market model of political freedom may remind some of the apparently similar models found in Nozick (1974, 297–334) and Kukathas (2003). Both feature a minimal political framework within which citizens found, enter, and leave voluntary associations of diverse kinds—cultural, religious, and so on—with the state's job being largely limited to ensuring peaceful coexistence (and friendly competition) among associations and protecting the right of citizens to exit from them. However, unlike my model, which is motivated by a desire to secure freedom as non-domination, these models are motivated by a specifically libertarian concern for freedom as non-interference, which explains why the exit rights they offer are entirely formal (Nozick 1974, 320–1, 333; Kukathas 2003, 107–14). As Kukathas himself states, his theory "does not place any great weight on choice, and emphasizes not so much the importance of decisions (to associate or dissociate) being voluntary as the value of their not being forced" (112). The "minimalist...view of the right of exit" found in both Nozick and Kukathas leads to worrying results, as associations would be permitted to "bring up children unschooled and illiterate...enforce arranged marriages... deny conventional medical care to their members (including children)...and...inflict cruel and 'unusual' punishment" (Kukathas 2003, 109, 134). Such FND-inconsistent associations would be ruled out by the much more substantive right of exit found in my model as well as by the ongoing constitutional and participatory restraints of the supplemental political model. In sharp contrast to my model, their models ignore and even exacerbate the fundamental problem of arbitrary power.

the ideal form of the economic model, as doing so will allow us to see much more clearly its unusual strengths, even if it requires us to overlook its weaknesses temporarily.

The perfectly competitive locational market ensured by the economic model is antipower in the precise sense spelled out by Pettit: specifically, participants in this market have no capacity to interfere with impunity and at will with the political interests of other participants. They enjoy no capacity to interfere at will because equilibrium tax and spending mixes across jurisdictions are set by the impersonal forces of supply (courtesy fiscal federalism) and demand (thanks to the frictionless mobility of citizens); consequently, there is no room for discretionary manipulation of these fiscal tools, either legal (e.g., exploitative taxes) or illegal (e.g., bribery), and therefore no leeway for the arbitrary exercise of political power. Any such attempt to deviate from these equilibrium mixes will lead to an exodus of citizens and, given fiscal federalism, the punishment of reduced revenues and fiscal insolvency; hence, participants also have no capacity to interfere with impunity. These features of a perfectly competitive locational market are antipower not just in Pettit's procedural sense but in his substantive sense as well, because they "track the interests" of the participants in at least one important way: under the admittedly counterfactual conditions of the ideal form of the economic model, interjurisdictional competition will generate a welfare optimum, securing both allocative efficiency (optimal sorting of citizens across jurisdictions) and productive efficiency (lowest-cost production of each jurisdiction's particular public-goods mix) and thereby making the shared political pie as large as possible—a result that is in the interest of all participants, differ as they may on how that pie should be divided up.[11]

Another way to see that competitive locational markets are antipower is to show that they bring about (equal) popular control of government. As Pettit argues, "if the citizenry control state discretion in a suitable manner—in a way that parallels your control over the person who holds the key to your alcohol cupboard—then the imposition of social order on those citizens will not take away from their freedom and will count as fully legitimate" (2012, 160). What is

---

[11] For a proof of this claim—the Tiebout Theorem—and the conditions under which it will hold, see Wooders 1989. This theorem is just the political equivalent of the First Welfare Theorem, first proved in Debreu 1959. Here would also be a good point to acknowledge the existence of a Tiebout (sub)literature that focuses almost exclusively on the productive-efficiency advantages of interjurisdictional competition: the so-called "competitive federalism" strand, including such seminal pieces as Buchanan (1996), Epstein (1992), Qian and Roland (1998), and Weingast (1995). Buchanan frankly acknowledges his use of a "Tiebout-like regime" (1996, 261), but others in this subliterature (e.g., Weingast 1995, 88) engage in more product differentiation without really showing that they have moved beyond the Tiebout framework.

required to make such control operative, though? Pettit identifies three preconditions for meaningful popular control of the state: individualization, unconditionality, and efficacy. I will describe each of these in turn, showing how the economic model meets them and thereby promotes political freedom:

1. **Individualization:** Pettit contends that "a system of control will have to guard against the domination of individual citizens, not just the domination of the collective citizenry," and will consequently have to grant "a comparable role to each of the individuals involved in the exercise of control" (2012, 167–8). He remarks that such individualized control might take two forms—a "personal" control in the form of an "individual veto" or "equal right of exit," or an equal share in a form of "joint" control—but he dismisses the possibility of the former for reasons to which I will return below. Notice, however, that the economic model we have been examining in this chapter offers control of the former, personal type. Such control is individualized in the strictest sense possible: each citizen has a unilateral power to change the kind of government under which he lives by simply moving to a new jurisdiction, and thanks to both resourced mobility and the numerous options available in a competitive locational market, he will be able to choose the form of government that he wants. Clearly, no system of joint control can offer this degree of individualization, even if it happens to be perfectly transparent, contestable, and impartial (2012, 209–18).
2. **Unconditionality:** Pettit also requires that this control be "unconditioned in the sense of being robust over changes in the will of the controlled government, or indeed of any party other than the controlling people" (2012, 167). In other words, the ability of the people to get the government to do what they want must not be dependent upon "the willingness of government to go along... [or] of the willingness of any other agency [like "an effectively independent army, a group of moneyed supporters, or even a foreign power"] to have the government go along" (2012, 172). He goes on to argue that such unconditionality will best be achieved if political society has a "resistive character," such that "government is likely to be resistance-averse, and... the people are likely to be resistance-prone" (2012, 218–29). The economic model gives society just such a resistive character, though not by the usual political means: the government is made resistance-averse not through a "mixed constitution" that divides powers but rather through fiscal federalism, which makes every jurisdiction as financially self-supporting as possible and thus anxious to retain residents and businesses; the people, on

the other hand, are rendered resistance-prone not by means of their virtuous vigilance and the collective agency of their social movements but rather by resourced mobility, which makes them willing and able to abandon abusive jurisdictions or credibly threaten to do so (ibid.).

3. **Efficacy:** Finally, Pettit insists that control "be effective or efficacious enough to impose a popular direction on government that nullifies the intrusion of alien will" from the likes of elected politicians, private lobbies, or unelected bureaucrats; their abuse is enabled by the "range of discretion" that accompanies the crafting, application, and interpretation of laws and policies (2012, 175–6, 229–38). Pettit offers a "tough-luck test" to judge whether such groups use their discretionary powers to take advantage of the citizenry: "the point of legitimacy is to ensure that you and your fellow citizens are not subject to an alien, controlling will, despite the fact that there may be a good deal of discretion exercised by those in power. Such legitimacy will be adequately ensured... to the extent that you and your fellows have good grounds to think that any unwelcome results of public decision-making are just tough luck" (177). Again, the economic model can be judged efficacious by this tough-luck test. As I pointed out earlier, discretionary power exercised within the Tiebout model is not arbitrary power because jurisdictions are constrained by both robust competition and mobile citizens, who choose from a continuum of communities differing by kind and degree of administrative discretion exercised inter alia. Because the number of viable jurisdictions has to be (substantially) less than the size of the overall population, it might be the case that citizens cannot find jurisdictions that perfectly match their ideal, whether in terms of administrative discretion, public goods, taxation, etc., but this need to settle for good-enough matches can be reasonably ascribed to tough luck rather than the machinations of some alien will.

As I acknowledged at the close of the last section, our economic model will fully possess these antipower characteristics only if all its assumptions are met, but there are many reasons to think they will not be: mobility will be far from frictionless, even if generously resourced; limits on the creation of new jurisdictions and on the capture of old ones (via "strong-mayor" systems or some species of receivership) will take the edge off interjurisdictional competition, etc. Before we summarily dismiss the economic model's antipower potential, though, we should realize that the alternative, political model to which it must be compared will itself fall short of its ideal form in a variety of ways, as Pettit frankly admits: even with participatory and constitutional checks in place, majoritarian tyranny will remain a danger, as will legislative gridlock, executive abuse of power, bureaucratic empire-building, judicial overreach, and interest-group rent-seeking (2012, 176, 211–13, 232–8). Moreover, because rational voters will grasp that the likelihood of casting the decisive vote is exceptionally small, they will invest little time and effort in becoming politically informed, making rational ignorance the norm and degrading the quality of democratic oversight in the process (Downs 1957, ch.13). Finally, the problem of free-riding behavior will make the formation of broad-based social movements a challenge and may limit their effectiveness as checks on arbitrary power (Olson 1971). So once we compare the economic and political models in the full light of their particular limitations, we will begin to understand the need for a mix of accountability mechanisms, one that takes into account their respective strengths and weaknesses and their tendency to vary by level of government. As I argued at the end of the last section, the economic model is at its strongest at the local and neighborhood level, though even there it must be supplemented by participatory and constitutional checks; as we move up the hierarchy of the federal system, it becomes decreasingly effective, leaving little but the political model to rely on at the national level. Regardless of its limitations, however, exit still has a vitally important role to play in promoting political freedom.

As I mentioned above, Pettit seems to deny this role to exit: he says that "citizens will not be able to think of themselves as exercising a personal control over the state.... [E]stablishing a general right of veto or exit would be inconsistent with the state's continued existence as a corporate agent that can reliably generate and implement law, since it would put it at the mercy of individual whim" (2012, 167–8; cf. 161–2, 165–6). Federal systems, however, call this claim into question, because they protect freedom of movement across their constituent self-governing sub-units—be they neighborhoods, cities, counties, provinces, or (within the European Union's Schengen Area) nation-states—without placing the legal authority of either the federation or its sub-units in jeopardy. In fact, our economic model demonstrates that resourced mobility, when combined with fiscal federalism, can help federations promote their citizens' welfare and reduce their vulnerability to domination. In this case, at least, exit enhances state capacities rather than threatening them. Interestingly, Pettit does recognize exit's potential to constrain domination in a different political context: he sees threats of "resistance," which he associates with "revolution or rebellion," as a means of disciplining the state and making popular control truly unconditional, and such resistance could be viewed as an illegal "exiting in place," an extraconstitutional check on the power of the state that might (paradoxically) be enabled through constitutional provisions, such as the US

Second Amendment (2012, 137–40, 173–4; Halbrook 1984). Pettit follows in the footsteps of the republican luminary John Locke here, as he is the first to recognize (Locke 1988, 406–28; Pettit 1997, 202, 2012, 173, 292). This conception of exit, however, remains within the bounds of the political model, working by analogy with constitutional checks and balances, and is profoundly different from the economic model's understanding of exit as resourced mobility within a perfectly competitive locational market.

There is one other way in which the economic model I have defended in this chapter may appear at odds with some of Pettit's claims. In *Republicanism*, Pettit is highly critical of interest-group pluralism, which he accuses of "backgrounding reason" in the following fashion: "it would argue that the best way to organize things in public life is to have a framework which means that things will happen according to reason—in particular, things will happen so as to produce maximum preference satisfaction—if people within that framework each look only to furthering their own interests" (1997, 203–4). In short, it reduces politics to economics, sidelining the public decision-makers who have to "make their decisions, and...make them transparently, on the basis of certain neutral considerations" and putting in their place an "invisible hand" that promotes the welfare of all by means of interest-group competition within a political marketplace (ibid.). This critique of interest-group pluralism looks like one that would apply equally well to my economic model. I would suggest, however, that Pettit's later writings offer a way to avoid this conclusion. In *On the People's Terms*, Pettit points out that "the influence exercised in control" need not be "active," i.e., involving "positive input on the part of the controller"; it may instead be "virtual," such that the controller is "poised to intervene, but only if the intervention is needed to keep the [system] on track" (2012, 156). That is, automatic stabilizers may be in place to keep a system in proper operating order, though these stabilizers may fail at times; so long as a controller has the power to intervene when such failures occur, we may think of him as being in virtual control of the system even when he is doing nothing. Pettit himself applies this insight to political "systems of shared control" that "include systems in which voting plays only a subsidiary part, or perhaps no part at all," as "we have seen that control may be exercised on the basis of...virtual influence" (2012, 168). Our economic model is just such a system: the combination of resourced mobility and fiscal federalism creates a framework within which individuals pursuing their own interests will unintentionally advance certain public ends (e.g., the general welfare, non-domination), but that framework is itself originally created and continuously monitored by popular controllers (or rather their representatives) who are empowered to intervene should the system fail to do its job. Pettit therefore has the theoretical resources available to incorporate our economic model into his preferred form of republicanism without serious tension.[12]

Even if this economic model can be successfully incorporated into Pettit's republicanism, however, the question remains of whether it should be, and more communitarian republicans are likely to think not.[13] In fact, Richard Dagger has explicitly criticized the Tiebout model, calling it a "cafeteria or shopping-mall conception of metropolis" and condemning its implicit treatment of politics as "merely another form of market activity" (Dagger 1997, 154). Dagger worries that the size, fragmentation, and especially high mobility associated with American cities jeopardize the preconditions of democratic self-government and thus of the reliable tracking of citizen interests and ideas. The power of exit, rather than being a way to check arbitrary power, is instead its principal enabler: mobility detaches and alienates citizens from the places where they live and converts them into "citizen-consumers" who shop for cities as they shop for clothes, unwisely depending upon the "supposedly apolitical professionals" who run cities to offer a wide range of public services at modest prices (154, 159). Only a small, stable urban environment with public-spirited citizens—something more closely resembling the city-state of classical antiquity than the sprawling, anonymous metropolis of modernity—can sustain republican liberty (155–6). He goes on to suggest a host of reform measures to create and sustain such urban environments, including greenbelt legislation, restrictions on expressways and intercity rail, "redistributing population" to "small, stable, well-defined cities," and using "the selective incentive of coercion to encourage men and women to join in community affairs" via "compulsory voting schemes" and mandatory community service (168–9). Dagger, in short, offers a vision of urban life that is a photographic negative of the Tiebout model: stability in place of flux, voice in place of exit, and civic duty in place of private freedom.[14]

Many if not most of Dagger's concerns here are reasonable ones, but I have doubts about whether they lead to his particular policy conclusions. For example, under current circumstances, I agree with Dagger that mobility is likely to have

---

[12] Also see Pettit's earlier work on active versus virtual discursive control (1995; 2001, 38–9, 76–7, 91–3). I set aside the question of whether Pettit should revise his critique of interest-group pluralism in light of what I have said here.

[13] I focus here on Dagger (1997, 154–72), but what he argues would almost certainly be seconded by Michael Sandel (1996, 2012), though admittedly he does not address the mobility issue directly. Interestingly, even Pettit complains that urban livability rankings "treat residents as consumers of cities... not properly as citizens" (2014, 109).

[14] The one point of overlap between the two is political decentralization, though in Dagger's model it serves to build familiarity and solidarity with fellow citizens rather than efficiency and a business-like responsiveness among urban managers (168–9).

some pernicious consequences, including ones that make certain forms of domination more likely. As he points out, the well-educated are most likely to move, yet they provide much civic leadership, and their flight from failing communities can accelerate their decline (163). Moreover, continuing and substantial fiscal subsidies to cities insulate them to some degree from the pressures of interjurisdictional competition, creating space for various kinds of discrimination, exploitation, and domination. I would contend, however, that the problem here is not the Tiebout model itself but rather a failure to secure its preconditions. As I have argued throughout the book, resourced exit and heightened competition are essential to making a market-oriented approach to curbing domination successful, and in the current context that would require better resourced mobility—especially for the poor and less educated—as well as a stricter fiscal federalism. So while it is true that, within a certain range of mobility, more of it can be counterproductive, the trick is to get beyond that range, and only by doubling down on a market-oriented approach can we do so.

Dagger, of course, has given us another approach. Rather than moving from a partial-exit to a free-exit world, he says that we should revert to something closer to a no-exit world: double down on where we live now, build community there, and fight forces that would undermine it. I admit to seeing the appeal of this strategy and can imagine situations where it would work, but I have concerns about its general applicability and even feasibility, especially in a modern, liberal society where citizens are rightly free (not) to associate, advocate, etc. For the sake of argument, though, let us assume that it is generally applicable and feasible. Is it desirable? I would maintain that it is not for the one group republicans should be most concerned about: the least advantaged. Poverty in the United States, as in many countries, is geographically concentrated, in our case in such places as the inner cities, rural Appalachia, and the Mississippi Delta. These communities have seen their most affluent, educated, and active citizens leave; it is simply too late to stop an exodus that has already occurred. Urging residents of these localities to build community where they live, even if it were promoted and resourced by state authorities, is unlikely to lead to major changes in their life prospects or those of their children: the jobs have gone and are not going to return, and folks left in the wake of deindustrialization and the decline of small-scale agriculture generally lack the skills and connections to effect such transformations. I think the best approach in these dire circumstances is the alternative outlined in this chapter: mobility vouchers, perhaps combined with "nudges" of the sort advocated by Thaler and Sunstein (e.g., allowing recipients of state aid to receive large advances on their support if they agree to move to one of America's innovation hubs)

(Moretti 2012, 163–4; Thaler and Sunstein 2009).[15] The results of the Move to Opportunity program I discussed above suggest that such vouchers would substantially improve the mental and physical health of adult recipients and the educational and employment prospects of their children (Kling et al. 2007; Chetty et al. 2015). Unattractive as it may be, the best solution to the problem of entrenched poverty and the ills, political and otherwise, that accompany it may be the resourced abandonment of the communities in question. This is an expensive proposition, to be sure, but given that the federal government alone spends over $13,000 each year per person in poverty—and even that figure only includes support via means-tested programs—much of this can be accomplished by reallocating rather than increasing spending (Haskins 2012, 1–2).

Having said all this, I agree with Dagger about one of his central claims: the importance of voice in constraining political domination. Even at the local level we cannot entirely dispense with participatory and constitutional approaches, and at the national level they are essentially the only tools at hand. Where I disagree is over the part that geographic exit, i.e., mobility, can play. As we have seen in the East German example and throughout the book, exit can act not simply as a substitute for voice but as a complement to it, empowering voice by increasing the credibility of citizen threats. Moreover, as we move down the hierarchy of federal institutions, it can take on a greater and greater role in curbing domination so long as it is properly resourced and combined with fiscal federalism. Far from being a danger to republican liberty, mobility is—or at least can be—its most important guarantor at the local and neighborhood level.

The importance of political voice at the national level raises a question that I sidestepped during my discussion of Hirschman in Chapter 1: what part, if any, does loyalty have to play in a republican theory? Hirschman defines loyalty as a "special attachment to an organization," such that it will discourage exit; in other words, he conceives of loyalty as an extra psychic barrier to exit, a price that must be paid to leave—and one that increases the more loyal one is (1970, 77). How important could loyalty be, then, at the national level, where exit is already quite costly and unlikely to occur? Critics of Hirschman have frequently complained about the narrowness of his conception of loyalty as psychic exit-barrier. Consider the following passage from Brian Barry's review of *Exit, Voice, and Loyalty*:

Loyalty does not normally mean a mere reluctance to leave a collectivity but rather *a positive commitment to further its welfare* by working for it, fighting for it, and—where one thinks it has gone astray—seeking to change it. Thus, voice (*as well as other forms of*

---

[15] A recent Obama housing-voucher initiative in Dallas nudges with both carrots and sticks: see Appelbaum 2015.

activity) is already built into the concept of loyalty. Reluctance to leave is not central.... We can check this by noticing that typically "disloyalty" is predicated of someone who acts contrary to the interests of the collectivity...while remaining a member of it. Someone who leaves is usually described as disloyal only if there is some special factor, for example that he has defected to another country carrying military secrets with him. (1974, 98; italics mine)

Barry's comments suggest two things. First, loyalty can be demonstrated not just by voice but by exit as well. Actions can speak louder than words, and escaping from a dysfunctional system can be intended to put additional pressure on that system in the hope of effecting change, especially if doing so sets an example for others and heightens public consciousness of the system's failure. The East German example is again pertinent: the image of Czechoslovak parking lots filled with the abandoned cars of fleeing East German citizens offered as eloquent a testimony to the GDR's moral bankruptcy as the image of protesters in the streets of Leipzig (see Sarotte 2014, 31 v. 73).

Second—and setting aside extreme cases such as East Germany, Cuba, North Korea, etc., for a moment—the importance of loyalty at the national level is difficult to understand unless we expand its meaning in the way that Barry recommends. Except where conditions are horrendous, citizens are unlikely to abandon their country in droves, meaning that exit will usually have little role to play at the national level. But this does not mean that loyalty, properly understood, has no role to play. In order for citizens to be willing to exercise voice at the national level, whether by protesting, lobbying, voting, or serving in public office (elective or otherwise), they must have a "positive commitment to further [their country's] welfare," at least where their voice is not being exercised for parochial purposes. Thus, in order to limit political domination at the national level, we must inculcate a sense of national loyalty via civic education both formal (e.g., civics classes) and informal (e.g., speeches, parades, wreath-laying ceremonies). The economic model presented in this chapter can go some way in compensating for deficits in democratic virtue at the local and neighborhood levels, but no such compensation is possible at the national level, and none will be for the near future.

The Limits and Potential of Political Freedom

Republicans have traditionally promoted political freedom by political means, relying on participatory and constitutional checks to avoid (or at least limit) arbitrary rule. Such efforts have borne impressive fruit: the foundation of constitutional democracies worldwide, beginning with Great Britain and the United States but spreading in waves over the past two centuries to every corner of the earth, is testimony to the power of republican ideas (Huntington 1993). What I have tried to show in this chapter is that another, economic model exists that promotes republican ends just as effectively, one that uses both federalism and the free movement across political sub-units that generally accompanies it to limit political power and thereby advance political freedom. This market-oriented approach to political republicanism can not just supplement but even substitute for the traditional political model, lessening our reliance on the vagaries of democratic control.

As I have also acknowledged throughout the chapter, though, such substitution can never be complete. Even at the local level the political model has a role to play, and as we move up the federal hierarchy that role becomes increasingly prominent. Indeed, the very political framework that makes the economic model possible can only be established through the exercise of voice at the national level: for instance, the mobility vouchers I have relied upon to make my case have to be a product of both political entrepreneurship and coalition-building in national politics. I have expended so much effort promoting this economic model not in order to reduce political freedom to market freedom but rather to show that, in order to minimize political domination, we must try to find an optimal mix of accountability mechanisms, one that will vary by level of government and even across time but will rarely if ever be all voice or all exit.

At the same time, we should also not underestimate the value of a distinctively economic approach to the problems of domination. Consider again the mobility vouchers that have played such an outsized role in this chapter's argument. These vouchers can do triple duty by restraining domination across the three spheres of family, market, and state: they can help wives escape their abusive husbands, workers flee their overbearing employers, and citizens exit their dysfunctional communities. Republican freedom demands that we minimize domination across the private and public realms, and the pairing of markets and mobility can create synergies over the whole range of human relations. More ambitiously, we can hope that in the years to come, the spread of open societies, advances in education, and reductions in transportation costs will make an application of the economic model to global society possible—a point to which I will return at book's end.

5

Republican Policy Pluralism

Over the last three chapters, I constructed a case for an economic model of republicanism that contrasts with the currently dominant political model, arguing that indirect empowerment of voice by means of enhanced competition and resourced exit is a safer and more effective way to curtail total domination (private plus public) than direct empowerment by either participatory or constitutional means. I conceded that this claim is more persuasive in the domestic and economic spheres than the political one but that, even there, a greater reliance on market-like mechanisms to constrain the exercise of arbitrary power by public agents would be advisable. Whether we are confronting domination in the family, market, or state, policy instruments that promote divorcive liberty can play a substantially greater role in advancing republican objectives than contemporary republicans have previously acknowledged.

This economic model would be accurately described as ideologically center-left. It entails an exit-oriented state interventionism, one that would require an activist government to enhance competition and resource exit from dominating relationships within markets of all types, be they marital, labor, or locational. The substantial intervention and redistribution required by such an approach make it leftist, while its tendency to work with rather than against the grain of markets makes it centrist. It is, in short, a contribution to progressive republican political thought, but one that is less social-democratic than market-democratic in character (cf. Tomasi 2012).

Republicans further to the right—e.g., center-right, limited-government republicans like Friedrich Hayek, whom I will discuss in greater detail below—might worry, however, that even if these interventions were well chosen and focused on indirectly enhancing voice as demanded by the economic model, public domination would remain an ever-present peril, especially as the state grew in size and power in order to secure the preconditions of effective exit. I have argued throughout this volume that social-democratic solutions to the problem of domination themselves risk exposing citizens to increased domination—or, setting aside this possibility, that they subdue private domination only at the cost of inadvertently enabling a lesser quantity of the public kind. Right-wing republicans might suggest, though, that even the more modest vision of exit-oriented state interventionism I have sketched may be susceptible to such charges, too, albeit to a reduced degree. If so, then the range of reasonable republican policy commitments might be wider than I have so far suggested, including not just an exit-oriented state interventionism but also a limited-government stance more commonly associated with classical liberalism than with republicanism.

A Right-Wing Critique of Exit-Oriented State Interventionism

Before we can explore the possibility of such a republican policy pluralism, however, we must first try to understand why right-wing republicans believe that even an exit-oriented policy strategy might run the risk of increasing domination. First, notice that many measures that would boost competition (e.g., antitrust action) or resource exit (e.g., welfare support) are open to abuse because their implementation would require discretionary power: antitrust authorities as well as welfare administrators require discretion in order to select targets for prosecution and determine eligibility for benefits, respectively, discretion that can be directed toward non-public objectives. Consider the European Commission's recent resumption of its antitrust case against Google, for example: the restart of this case was done at the discretion of the new competition commissioner, Margrethe Vestager, and bears the telltale signs of being driven more by the uncompetitiveness of rival European platforms than the anticompetitive behavior of Google (*The Economist* 2015). Antitrust powers necessarily rely upon a prosecutorial discretion that can be used just as readily to shield firms from foreign competition or burnish the reputation of a prosecutor with ambitions for higher office as it can to safeguard consumers from predatory business practices or workers from monopsonistic employers.

Even more troubling—especially for a prioritarian republicanism stressing the security of the most vulnerable citizens (Lovett 2010, 201; Pettit 2012, 89–90)—is the kind of discretionary power that is often placed in the hands of welfare administrators. Nearly all state redistribution is conditional, whether on educational enrolment (e.g., job retraining), looking for work, work itself (e.g., the Earned Income Tax Credit or "workfare"), or other policy objectives (e.g., immunizing and educating children, as with conditional cash transfers in Mexico, Brazil, and elsewhere) (*The Economist* 2013). Verifying that the poor meet these conditions requires that discretionary power be given to welfare agents, both to determine whether the conditions are being met (*assessment*, including investigatory powers of various sorts) and to cut off aid if they fail to be met (*redress*). Certain limitations can be put on such powers, such as rights of appeal to quasi-judicial bodies if benefits are cut, but there will remain an ineliminable degree of bureaucratic discretion that can and inevitably will be used for non-public purposes, be they financial (e.g., bribery), tribal (e.g., protecting the bureaucratic-class interests of welfare officials), or ideological (e.g., punishing or "liberating" the poor, depending on the official's political leaning). The state's dominant position in the charity market, which is guaranteed not only by its size and scope but also by the fact that public charity tends to "crowd out" private charity, will only make this problem worse.[1] Welfare officials will have a degree of arbitrary power over recipients that private benefactors rarely do.

Republicans are well aware that benefit conditionality and its accompanying bureaucratic discretion can compromise the poor's freedom (as non-domination)—even when the condition in question is just a means test (i.e., an income-based eligibility rule). As Frank Lovett argues:

> It is doubtful whether means testing can be carried out in a suitably non-arbitrary manner: practical experience suggests that state welfare agencies must inevitably employ extensive bureaucratic discretion in carrying out such policies, and that the particular vulnerability of persons in need of public assistance renders the usual sorts of constraints on such discretion more or less ineffective. From a domination-minimizing point of view, it will not do to replace the arbitrary charity of private individuals and groups with the arbitrary charity of state welfare agencies, for this would merely substitute one form of domination for another. (2010, 198–9; cf. Pettit 1997, 162 and White 2003)

Both he and Pettit have therefore advocated an *unconditional* basic income (UBI), which would dispense with the need for such bureaucratic discretion (Lovett 2010, 199–203; Pettit 2007).

One problem with such an approach, however, is that administrative discretion would not only continue to be exercised in other realms (e.g., antitrust actions) but might even be amplified in those realms in unintended ways *because* of its reduction in the realm of public charity. To see why this might be the case, first notice how colossally expensive it would be to implement even a modest UBI. In the USA, for instance, a $5000 per year UBI—which is not even halfway to the poverty threshold for a single person—would consume nearly half the

---

[1] A series of articles (starting with Andreoni 1993) has found evidence of substantial but incomplete crowding out of voluntary contributions to public goods, such as charity, by tax financing. Lovett notes this effect but does not see its implications for bureaucratic domination (2010, 206n30).

federal budget (Health and Human Services 2015).² Even if we were to take into account certain compensating reductions in other entitlement programs, such a UBI would necessitate a substantial increase in taxation, and this very push to raise more revenue would itself increase state domination. The reason for this is simple: higher taxes, *ceteris paribus*, will lead to more tax evasion; therefore, more discretionary powers will have to be granted to revenue agents for enforcement purposes, whether to discover evaders by requisitioning documents, interrogating suspects, and so on (*assessment*) or to impose penalties (*redress*).³ As with the antitrust and welfare officials I discussed earlier, revenue agents will be able to use this enhanced discretion in pursuit of non-public ends—and even if they never in fact did so, the vulnerability of citizens subject to such authority would make them quite likely to fail what Pettit calls the "eyeball test," i.e., the ability to "look others in the eye without reason for the fear or deference that a power of interference might inspire" (2012, 84). Even IRS agents with adamantine professional integrity will inspire fear and deference because it is their *ability* to abuse, not actual abuse, that constitutes domination: as Pettit says, "the grievance I have in mind is that of having to live at the mercy of another" (1997, 4–5; also, see Dewan 2014 on IRS use of civil-forfeiture laws, which has struck fear into the hearts of many small-business owners).

Even if we ultimately decided that these increases in public domination could be justified by the even greater reductions in private domination that they brought about, we would still have to worry about the long-term consequences of such a choice. The more powerful the government becomes—the more that it can command persons and resources through taxation, regulation, and so forth—the more attractive a target it becomes for capture by rent-seeking interest groups, who can then use its power for non-public ends such as preventing the entry of competitors, enforcing cartel-pricing arrangements, and obtaining tax breaks and subsidies. The more authority the state is given, even for initially beneficial ends, the more it can be redirected by organized interests to dominate and exploit unorganized interests, and this is true whether these organized

---

² My calculation here is for 2013. The total US population in 2013 was 316,497,531 (US Census Bureau 2015). (Many basic-income supporters include children, so I use total population: see van Parijs 2006, 7.) Multiplying this by $5000 gives a figure of about $1.582 trillion. Total federal spending in 2013 was approximately $3.5 trillion, so a UBI of this size would have eaten up a bit over 45 percent of the budget that year (Congressional Budget Office 2014).

³ A long series of books and articles (including Ali et al. 2001; Cebula 2004; Clotfelter 1983; Feige 1994; Klepper et al. 1991; Tanzi 1982) has confirmed that tax evasion is an increasing function of tax rates. Lovett maintains that "JMD [Justice as Minimizing Domination] demands that we set the [UBI] as high as we possibly can," but he does not include the resulting increase in domination by revenue agents in his calculus (2010, 202–3).

interests are hijacking old powers or acquiring new ones by bargaining with legislators and regulators, whom they can offer bribes, campaign contributions, and post-government jobs as inducements. As one of the originators of regulatory-capture theory, George Stigler, states in his seminal article on the subject: "as a rule, regulation is acquired by the industry and is designed and operated primarily for its benefit" (Stigler 1975, 114; cf. Laffont and Tirole 1991 and Levine and Forrence 1990). The Interstate Commerce Commission (ICC) and Civil Aeronautics Board (CAB) were for many decades the canonical examples of regulatory capture in action: these agencies controlled routes, entry, and pricing in the railroad, trucking, and airline industries and did so, not in the interest of consumers, but in the interest of the producers themselves (see Huntington 1952 on the ICC and McCraw 1986, ch. 7, on the CAB). Their abuses were so egregious that both of them were ultimately abolished (the ICC in 1995 and the CAB in 1985), but not before a century and a half-century, respectively, of state-enforced cartelization had elapsed. As extreme as these two cases are, less extreme examples are ubiquitous in the annals of tax and regulatory policymaking (e.g., the European antitrust case against Google that I mentioned earlier), and though it is the case that concerted efforts by public-spirited journalists, advocacy groups, and legislators can reduce such behavior (e.g., by exposure of "pay-to-play" schemes and adoption of campaign-finance reform), the enormous, varied, and consequently difficult-to-monitor powers of the modern administrative state combined with the inevitable corruptions of democratic politics will continue to make rent-seeking an attractive activity. This ugly political reality should at least make us pause before we rush to increase state power in response to private domination. The twentieth century was a time of accelerating growth in the size and powers of the state, with each new crisis (war, depression, etc.) ratcheting them up ever higher, and whether such growth served to diminish or enlarge total domination is a matter of debate (Higgs 1987).

The picture I have just painted is a stark one, of course, presented for effect and reflecting a classical-liberal narrative about the state that right-wing republicans also ratify. Although I find the narrative persuasive at certain points, I also think it is unconvincing in this extreme form and too skeptical of the possibility of ameliorative state action, including those actions demanded by my economic model of republicanism. Consider the following two points. First, the state may be able to redistribute income in a way that avoids or at least minimizes the negative side effects of conditionality. For example, Social Security makes receipt of payments age-conditional without risking domination, largely because these conditions are readily verifiable through public records and therefore not vulnerable to manipulation by bribe-seeking or otherwise abusive officials. To a lesser extent, the same may be said of the Earned Income Tax Credit and other wage subsidies, whose work conditions can be checked through the ordinary tax-reporting system. (Contrast this with big public-employment schemes of the kind used in India, for instance, where the scope for abuse is much larger.) Much depends upon how specific government programs are designed and implemented, and republicans could design them to minimize the risk of domination. Second, the state might also be able to raise revenue in a way that avoids or at least minimizes the possibility of domination by revenue agents. For instance, payroll withholding for income taxes has reduced such domination by having firms act as middlemen between the state and citizen, redirecting the IRS's discretionary power from vulnerable citizens to better-insulated corporate bureaucracies. A fair assessment of the effects of state intervention on total domination will reveal a more nuanced picture than that painted by classical liberals and their republican sympathizers.

However, my judgment that the beliefs of right-wing republicans are incorrect (or at least overstated) does not imply that they are unreasonable. As I will suggest below, their ideas cannot be so easily dismissed, because they are part of a range of reasonable historical and policy views. The conclusion we should therefore draw from them is not that a minimal state is best, but rather that a minimal state *might* be best, contingent upon our beliefs about the threat of private versus public domination. Neo-republicans, in short, should adopt a comparative-institutional approach (Stigler 1975, ch. 7): they should recognize that states as well as markets can be dominating, that perfect states are no more likely than perfect markets, and therefore that escalating efforts to counteract private power with public power will at some point increase rather than decrease total domination, which is the very thing neo-republicans are trying to minimize.

The Burdens of Judgment and Reasonable Policy Pluralism

The central question, then, is: **what extent of public power minimizes total domination?** Or to make the continuous dichotomous for the sake of simplicity: is total domination minimized with a minimal state or rather with a more extensive state, one guided by the sort of exit-oriented policy strategy that I have advanced throughout this book? I am asking this question not in order to provide a definitive answer—that would be too ambitious for the modest scope of this chapter or even this book—but rather to show that different answers to this question can be reasonable in light of the "burdens of judgment" under which all conscientious deliberators operate. Again, my own judgment is that an exit-oriented state interventionism best minimizes total domination, but I also acknowledge the difficulty of the question at hand and consider it worthy of further study.

When trying to answer a question such as this, we necessarily bear Rawlsian "burdens of judgment," constituted by "the many hazards involved in the correct (and conscientious) exercise of our powers of reason and judgment in the ordinary course of political life" (Rawls 1993, 56). The first three hazards Rawls discusses are especially relevant in our case; he describes them as follows:

a. The evidence—empirical and scientific—bearing on the case is conflicting and complex, and thus hard to assess and evaluate.
b. Even where we agree fully about the kinds of considerations that are relevant, we may disagree about their weight, and so arrive at different judgments.
c. To some extent all our concepts, and not only moral and political concepts, are vague and subject to hard cases; and this indeterminacy means that we must rely on judgments and interpretations (and on judgments about interpretations) within some range (not sharply specifiable) where reasonable persons may differ (ibid.).[4]

Each of these hazards has an important bearing on how different neo-republicans will answer the question of how extensive public power should be. Even when assessing the same evidence, they will invariably differ amongst themselves about which approach better reduces total domination. Among the causes of disagreement will be their divergent assessments of the nature and extent of private domination, the efficacy of government responses to such domination, and the possibility of keeping the state and its agents constrained by truly public purposes as state power expands.

---

[4] In the main text I ignore the last three hazards he discusses, as they are less relevant to our case. Hazard (d), which as with the first three applies "mainly to the theoretical use of our reason," is that due to the unavoidable diversity of modern life, "citizens' total experiences are disparate enough for their judgments to diverge, at least to some degree, on many if not most cases of any significant complexity" (1993, 56–7). Because my focus here is on neo-republican political philosophers, this consideration appears less relevant: due to similar educations and career trajectories, their "total experiences" are likely to overlap considerably, though differences in family, gender, race, etc., will continue to produce divergences. Hazards (e) and (f), by contrast, are of a moral character: hazard (e) is that "often there are different kinds of normative considerations of different force on both sides of an issue and it is difficult to make an overall assessment," and hazard (f) is that, due to a "limited social space," we are "forced to select among cherished values... [and consequently] face great difficulties in setting priorities and making adjustments" (57). Because neo-republicans all share an overriding commitment to minimizing domination defined in a particular way, these hazards again seem less relevant.

Consider first the nature and extent of private domination. As I have remarked numerous times throughout the book, it is the ability to abuse, not actual abuse, that constitutes domination: those who have a "capacity to interfere with impunity and at will in certain choices that the other is in a position to make" dominate that person, even if they decide never to exercise that capacity (Pettit 1996, 578). Consequently, when we are trying to evaluate the nature and extent of private domination, we cannot simply count up instances of abuse; instead, we must assess the structural aspects of relationships to determine whether they involve domination, and such assessments can and typically will vary substantially across different assessors. Recall my discussion in Chapter 3 of levels of labor-market competitiveness, ranging from perfect competition to monopsony. Even for a given labor market, empirical estimates of employer power are likely to differ for a number of innocent reasons, including the investigator's choice of a foundational theoretical model (from among the many rival models of oligopsony, for example) and its econometric specification, the variety and quality of data with which to test it (e.g., are close substitutes available for employers and/or employees?), etc. Relatedly, how should we weigh the relative danger of employer versus employee power in such markets? Ideally, this decision would be data-driven, but given that the empirical evidence is likely to be "conflicting and complex," as Rawls says, we may be forced to fall back on broad readings of labor history or more systematic theoretical considerations (about, for example, the relative bargaining power of different socioeconomic classes) in order to assign weights. Reasonable assessors will disagree about these readings and theoretical considerations, however, and so we should expect differences in weights assigned and conclusions reached. We should also keep in mind differences of opinion about conceptual matters, such as the meaning of domination and its definitional components, and the effects these might have on our judgments regarding the nature and extent of private domination. For example, Pettit's definition of power, which I reproduced earlier in the paragraph, associates it with "impunity." I argued in Chapter 3 that *competitive* labor markets, at least, punish abusive employer behavior with a loss of workers and profits, but some republicans may deny that this is punishment, strictly speaking, because it fails to meet certain essential criteria (e.g., being imposed by a public enforcer according to rules that citizens have understood and explicitly endorsed, either in person or through their legislative representatives) and would therefore "background, not foreground, reason" (Pettit 1997, 203). I responded to such concerns in Chapters 3 and 4, but they are based upon a reasonable alternative interpretation of Pettit's definition, one that would have ramifications not simply for the narrow question at hand but indeed for my entire economic model of republicanism.

Turn now to the efficacy of government responses to private domination and the prospect of such responses increasing rather than decreasing total domination. A major theme of this book has been that social-democratic policies, be they participatory or constitutional, are unlikely to be effective and that even if they are they will generally be less effective than exit-oriented policies, which should therefore be a preferred approach of republicans to limiting total domination. As I discussed earlier, however, even an exit-oriented strategy has its risks, assessments of which will vary among reasonable observers. First, reasonable people will differ regarding the effectiveness of these policies, again owing to the "conflicting and complex" empirical evidence; for example, labor economists continue to disagree about the efficacy of minimum-wage laws as a mechanism for checking exploitation and redistributing income to the most vulnerable workers, though most are skeptical (see Card and Krueger 1997 and Neumark and Wascher 2008). Even if we assume that such policies are effective at reducing private domination, we still have to worry about their tendency to increase public domination by bolstering the administrative discretion of the police, antitrust officials, welfare bureaucrats, and revenue agents, but even impartial observers will put different weights on the relative risks here, weights that will be informed in part by the empirical evidence but also by certain historical and theoretical concerns. For instance, some assessors will worry more about private power, in light of the rising influence of corporations and the tendency of the capitalist class to utilize its political pull for self-enrichment, than about public power, due not only to the public spiritedness of state employees but also to the success of various forms of oversight (administrative, judicial, and legislative) in making their actions track "the welfare and world-view of the public" (Pettit 1997, 56). Others, however, will be more concerned with public power than private: the state, after all, claims a monopoly on the use of physical coercion, and no degree of governmental oversight can guarantee that such coercive powers will only be deployed for public purposes (Pettit 2012, 176; Lovett and Pettit 2009, 23–4); private power, by contrast, is forever vulnerable to unpredictable shifts in the competitive landscape and distribution of wealth and is therefore less to be feared. Throw competing narratives about twentieth-century expansion of public power into the mix—was it a liberating force that freed us from the tyranny of private capital or an oppressive force that threatened our civil and economic liberties?—and you will see why we should expect even neo-republicans to differ, sometimes dramatically, regarding our key question: what extent of public power minimizes total domination?

Michael Sandel versus Friedrich Hayek

Such intramural disagreement is nicely illustrated by the conflicting political programs of Michael Sandel and Friedrich A. Hayek, both of whom can be understood as republican political theorists. Sandel explicitly endorses republicanism in *Democracy's Discontent* (1996), in which he argues for a "republican theory [that, unlike interest-group pluralism,] does not take people's existing preferences, whatever they may be, and try to satisfy them. It seeks instead to cultivate in citizens the qualities of character necessary to the common good of self-government" (25). He views private domination, whether of employees by employers or of the poor by the rich, as the greatest barrier to the cultivation of these distinctively republican virtues. For example, he offers a highly sympathetic portrayal of mid-nineteenth-century labor republicans, who complained of being "wage slaves" and bristled at the "purse-proud insolence" of their employers (1996, 153, 172–4; cf. Gourevitch 2014). More recently, he has reminded us that "market choices are not free choices if some people are desperately poor or lack the ability to bargain on fair terms," which he claims is the case with transactions as various as ticket scalping and kidney sales (2012, 36, 112). These abuses at the hands of powerful private actors call for state action in defense of equality, he avers, because "the republican tradition teaches that severe inequality undermines freedom by corrupting the character of both rich and poor and destroying the commonality necessary to self-government" (1996, 330). In these ways, at least, Sandel's republicanism overlaps with the exit-oriented economic model that I offered in prior chapters, which also sought to limit the abuses of monopsonistic and oligopsonistic employers and empower the most vulnerable in diverse market settings, and it consequently appears to be within the range of reasonable republican views on the danger of private domination and the desirability of state action to counter it.

Unfortunately, this initial appearance is deceptive, and upon closer examination Sandel's views are at variance with an exit-oriented state interventionism and closer to social-democratic approaches that I have consistently targeted for criticism. First, Sandel grounds his republicanism on participation rather than non-domination: "republican political theory teaches that to be free is to share in governing a political community that controls its own fate" (1996, 274; cf. 202). This definitional commitment to what I have called the political model leads unsurprisingly to a very laudatory portrait of labor-republican advocates of a "cooperative commonwealth," one in which "the wage system" would be replaced, by means of both "political action" and "strikes and trade unions," with "a scheme of cooperatives in which workers would share in the profits of labor and govern themselves" (1996, 186–8, 190). As I argued in Chapters 1 and 3, however, these social-democratic responses to the problem of private domination risk increasing overall domination, whether by enhancing the quasi-public power of labor cartels or of the state itself in its pursuit of industrial democracy or even associational socialism. The narrowness of Sandel's republicanism excludes the economic model by definitional legerdemain, hiding from us the possibility that the very private domination he condemns might best be addressed by resourcing exit and enhancing competition in labor markets. Participation, after all, is just one means among others to the true end of republicanism, viz., freedom as non-domination, and one more appropriate in the political realm than in the domestic and economic realms.

More troubling than this social-democratic commitment to universal participation across social spheres—to what Nancy Rosenblum has called "congruence" (1989, 38–40)—is Sandel's pronounced suspicion of economic exchange and commercial society more broadly. We can see it in his condemnation of consumerism, where he says in a Rousseauean vein that "consumption, when it figured at all in republican political economy, was a thing to be moderated, disciplined, or restrained for the sake of higher ends. An excess of consumption, or luxury, was often seen as a form of corruption, a measure of the loss of civic virtue" (1996, 224–5). This worry leads quite naturally to his more recent "corruption objection" to markets: "we corrupt a good, an activity, or a social practice whenever we treat it according to a lower norm than is appropriate to it" (2012, 46, 110). He raises this objection in a dizzying array of settings, ranging from surrogacy markets to programs that incentivize childhood reading and obesity reduction (2012, 59, 61, 71). Sandel's solution to these evils of market corruption—as well as to what he takes to be the related evils of unfairness in exchange to which I alluded above—is what Michael Walzer refers to as "blocked exchanges," i.e., state regulations that prohibit certain sorts of trade (Walzer 1983, 100–3).

Such regulatory intervention, though, is vulnerable to criticism on the republican grounds of anti-paternalism and anti-moralism. If certain instances of economic exchange are truly unfree because some participants "are desperately poor or lack the ability to bargain on fair terms," then the solution is not to block the exchanges but rather to empower those participants by providing them with material resources or by heightening competition in the relevant markets (2012, 112). Blocking these exchanges without seeking to empower their disadvantaged participants not only prevents them from making the most of a bad situation—in a second-best world, being exploited may be better than *not* being exploited (e.g., sweat-shop labor may be preferable to the available alternatives, such as unemployment)—but obstinately insists on treating the unsightly symptoms instead of the underlying disease, which is asymmetric power relations. If, on the other hand, the disadvantaged participants are properly empowered, then blocking such exchanges would qualify as an unwarranted paternalism: so long as all participants are sufficiently informed and resourced and no spillovers happen, the state has no business forbidding "capitalist acts between consenting adults" (Nozick 1974, 163). To quote Frank Lovett on this point:

> The most reliable and least intrusive way to discourage people from trading away their freedom from domination is to have the public meet the basic needs of those unable to do so for themselves. Not having to trade away their freedom from domination in order to meet their basic needs, few would probably choose to do so.... Moreover, unlike either the blocked exchange or the regulatory approach, this approach would continue to respect the choices that people make, and thus not fall afoul the paternalism objection. (2010, 198; cf. Pettit 2012, 98)

As for Sandel's belief that some kinds of economic exchange are inherently "corrupting," in that they "treat [the thing exchanged] according to a lower norm than is appropriate to it," it is simply a blatant form of moralism and, as such, inconsistent with republican neutrality towards (justice-respecting) conceptions of the good, a trait it shares with some species of liberalism (e.g., Rawls 1993, 190–4).[5] As Pettit confirms:

> Like the liberal project, our proposal—our republican proposal—is motivated by the assumption that the ideal is capable of commanding the allegiance of the citizens of developed multicultural societies, regardless of their more particular conceptions of the good.... [I]n seeking a relatively neutral brief for the state—a brief that is not tied to any particular conception of the good—republicanism joins with liberalism against communitarianism. (1997, 96, 120; cf. Lovett 2010, 162)[6]

---

[5] Another, related difficulty with Sandel's position is that, assuming that the allegedly corrupting exchanges occur in properly competitive markets, their inconsistency with "appropriate" norms may call into question not the exchanges but rather the norms themselves. Competitive markets are, among other things, tools for sustaining domination-free relationships, so if these norms call for blocking exchanges within such markets, they obstruct the republican goal of minimizing domination and should therefore be reformed or rejected. On this point, see Brennan and Jaworski 2015.

[6] More recent work by Lovett might appear to call into question these claims about republican neutrality, but in truth it does not. Lovett believes that republicans may be permitted or even required to favor conceptions of the good that make room for civic virtue, patriotism, etc., as these are by assumption necessary for the success of republicanism; otherwise, states might become dominating because they are inadequately monitored, resisted, etc., by their citizens. He suggests that this favoritism could be inconsistent with neutrality. But even liberal theories of justice like that of Rawls stipulate that their support for neutrality applies only to *justice-respecting* conceptions of the good; no theory of justice, republican or liberal, can be neutral with respect to the preconditions of its own efficacy. It is therefore no surprise when Rawls states that "even though political liberalism seeks common ground and is neutral in aim, it is important to emphasize that it may still affirm the superiority of certain forms of moral character and encourage certain moral virtues. Thus, justice as fairness includes an account of certain political virtues—the virtues of fair social cooperation such as

Sandel's attack on surrogacy markets, for example, hinges upon his controversial conviction that "trafficking in the right to procreate promotes a mercenary attitude towards children that corrupts parenthood," but this view is not widely shared and seems dependent on a specific, rather hazily-sketched conception of the good (2012, 71); if so, it moralistically violates republican neutrality. In short, for Sandel to bring his political theory within the broad church of reasonable republican views on domination, he would need to repent his atavistic hostility to markets and commercial society, make peace with republican neutrality, and embrace an exit-oriented, not a participation-and-regulation-oriented, state interventionism.

Unlike Sandel, Hayek constructs his political theory on the same foundation of freedom as non-domination as Pettit and other neo-republicans do—and this despite the fact that he thinks of himself as a classical liberal rather than a republican. In *The Constitution of Liberty* (1960), he starts by defining freedom as "the state in which a man is not subject to coercion by the arbitrary will of another or others" (11). Hayek contrasts such at-will interference with the lawful coercion of a state that governs by "known general rules" and imposes "limited and foreseeable duties"; such coercion is legitimate because it is "independent of the arbitrary will of another person" and therefore "impersonal" in nature (21). Pettit recognizes the kinship here but nonetheless says that Hayek's conception of freedom "falls short of freedom as non-domination, since it is consistent with allowing domination... within those spaces where the relevant legal injunction leaves people to other devices. Thus it is consistent... with domination occurring in the workplace or the home or in any of a multitude of so-called private spaces" (1997, 89–90). Pettit fails to substantiate this claim, however, and it is not supported by Hayek's writings, which do in fact concern themselves with the problem of private domination within the interstices of rule-governed public power. For example, Hayek worries that, due to the class origins and allegiances of judges, the common law will become increasingly biased over time in favor of dominant classes (e.g., landlords, creditors, and businesses), an injustice that threatens the impartiality and non-arbitrariness of law and must consequently be corrected via legislation by the people's representatives (1982, Vol. 1, 89). Even more strikingly, he considers the growing size and power of corporations a threat to competition, and he responds to those who believe that "freedom of contract"

---

the virtues of civility and tolerance, of reasonableness and the sense of fairness" (1993, 194). Consequently, favoring conceptions of the good that make room for civic virtue and patriotism can be entirely consistent with republican neutrality. (For further details on this recent work, see Lovett and Whitfield 2016.)

should be uncritically extended from natural to artificial persons by noting that "it may on occasion be the duty of government to protect the individual against organized groups," as when corporations sign contracts in restraint of trade and thereby injure consumers (1948, 115–16).

Having said this, Hayek worries more about the private power of unions than businesses and more about public domination than private; that is, he assigns very different weights to these threats to freedom than someone like Sandel does. Hayek points to extraordinary legal privileges that have been granted to labor combinations, such as "the use of the picket line as an instrument of intimidation," closed and union shops that violate the right to work, and immunity against tort claims (1960, 274–5, 278–9). The private power created by these privileges allows labor cartels to dominate not just employers but even fellow workers, including but certainly not limited to those made unemployed by the cartels' acts in restraint of trade (1960, 269–72). Hayek's emphasis on union power may seem outdated, given the secular decline in union membership, but that fall has taken place even while public-sector unionization has surged: in 2014, public-sector workers had a union-membership rate five times that of private-sector ones (35.7 percent v. 6.6 percent) (Bureau of Labor Statistics 2015). Apart from the expansion in the number of so-called "right-to-work" states, the legal privileges enumerated by Hayek still exist and continue to sustain pockets of private power in labor markets, regardless of whether employers in them have any market power themselves.

Hayek's unease regarding the private power of unions becomes outright anxiety when he turns to the increasing risk of state domination. To be clear, Hayek's worry here is distinct from the libertarian one: as a classical liberal, he supports a rudimentary welfare state, including such exit-oriented state interventions as educational vouchers for underprivileged children and even a decent social-minimum income (1960, 257–9; 1982, Vol. 1, 141–2, Vol. 2, 84, 87, Vol. 3, 55). He is apprehensive, however, about the possibility that the public—or, more likely, pressure groups with rent-seeking purposes—will push the state to move beyond this limited social agenda under the banner of equality of opportunity or distributive justice, which he thinks would endanger the very foundations of the liberal social order (1982, Vol. 2, 84–8). To quote Hayek on this point:

No system of rules of just individual conduct, and therefore no free action of the individuals, could produce results satisfying a principle of distributive justice.... The fact is simply that we consent to retain, and agree to enforce, uniform rules for a procedure which has greatly improved the chances of all to have their wants satisfied, but at the price of all individuals and groups incurring the risk of unmerited failure. (1982, Vol. 2, 69–70; cf. Nozick 1974, 160–4)

Despite social justice being a mirage, the attempt to achieve it will allow the state to accumulate discretionary powers that will become a danger to individual freedom; the regulatory capture that I discussed earlier means that interest groups will hijack these powers in order to serve their own selfish ends and lobby bureaucrats and legislators for additional ones (1982, Vol. 2, 138–9, Vol. 3, 10). For these reasons, Hayek endorses principled opposition to any expansion of state power beyond that necessary for a minimal welfare state, even when such an expansion is ostensibly for beneficial ends like reducing private domination or advancing the general welfare.

Again, I find some of Hayek's points persuasive but his overall assessment unconvincing. As I noted at the end of Chapter 3, unionization can be justified under certain circumstances as a second-best response to collusion among employers and lack of legal agency among employees. Enhancing competition in and resourcing exit from such labor markets would be better, but these policies may be politically infeasible, in which case the sort of rigid opposition to union privilege offered by Hayek would make the best the enemy of the good. Similarly, while Hayek is right to worry about regulatory capture, he both understates the threat of private domination by business interests and overstates the risk of public domination by state administrators, whose discretionary powers can often be limited by good institutional design, as I argued earlier. Although Pettit goes too far in saying that Hayek's conception of freedom is "consistent...with domination occurring in the workplace or the home or in any of a multitude of so-called private spaces" (1997, 89–90), he is right in believing that Hayek focused too much on public rather than private domination, an overemphasis that is in part an understandable reaction to mid-twentieth-century Nazi and Soviet totalitarianism.

My task here, though, is not to fully evaluate such ideas but rather to suggest that there is a case for extending the range of reasonable republican views on domination to the right, even as we move to exclude those social-democratic views at the other end of this range. The bulk of my book has been a defense of exit-oriented state interventionism and a critique of social-democratic policies that try to empower voice directly, via participatory and constitutional routes, rather than indirectly, by the less risky and more efficient path of enhanced competition and resourced exit. I do concede, however, that the thesis of right-wing republicans such as Hayek—viz., that even the relatively modest exit-oriented policy strategy might lead to increased domination—is worthy of further study and investigation. By contrast, the recent efforts of certain neo-republicans to drive the doctrine ever further to the left (e.g., Gourevitch 2013 and 2014) are less likely to be fruitful, partly because they rely upon a conception of freedom more focused on "structural domination" than on domination proper and thus beyond republicanism. To draw on Sharon Krause's work: insofar as unequal ownership of the means of production is the result of a process that is "largely unconscious and unintentional," the product of innumerable accidents of birth and lifestyle and myriad decentralized contractual arrangements, the mere fact that some people are capitalists and some are workers does not constitute domination; something more is required, such as collusive behavior by capitalists in markets or in politics that allows them to acquire arbitrary power over workers (Krause 2013, 2; cf. Pettit 2006b, 139).[7] The proper response to this, however, is not the socialist "labor republicanism" advocated by Gourevitch and Sandel, but rather the exit-oriented method advanced throughout this book. The economic model of republicanism remains the only strategy that answers republicanism's distinctive call to end arbitrary interference by private *and* public actors in the lives of citizens.

---

[7] I do not mean to imply by this that there is nothing morally objectionable about unequal ownership of the means of production, especially if it is severe and enduring. It might be unfair or even constitute a distributive injustice, which is Rawls's view: see Rawls 2001, Part IV, on property-owning democracy as a way of realizing justice as fairness. It might even be considered a sort of oppression: see Krause 2013 and Young 1990, 37. All I want to claim here is that these concerns are different from the distinctively republican concern with domination.

Conclusion

If we have learned anything about the state over the past quarter of a millennium, it is that constitutional democracy, whatever its flaws, is more effective than any other political system at preventing the exercise of arbitrary power by public agents. Combining democratic participation, both formal and informal, with institutional checks and balances allows the people to hold their rulers to account but simultaneously restrains popular power, keeping both rulers and ruled from becoming tyrants. Given the success of this republican strategy in the political realm, it is wholly unsurprising that contemporary republicans would try to extend it to other realms too. Reasoning by analogy, they have endorsed both participatory and constitutional solutions to the problem of private power. As I have argued throughout the book, though, this analogy is a weak one: due to the relative ease of exiting family and firm, the domestic and economic realms are fundamentally unlike the political one—and even in the political realm, exit is often feasible, increasingly so as we approach the local level. This essential difference implies that the political model so beloved by neo-republicans is not a universal strategy for dealing with arbitrary power but rather a special strategy for specific social contexts. Insofar as a universal strategy exists, it is the one suggested by a different analogy: that between the economic realm, on the one hand, and the domestic and political realms, on the other. Markets of varying kinds exist in all three—spousal markets, labor markets, locational markets, and so forth—and when the state intervenes to make them properly competitive and to help their participants enter and exit them at will, it creates environments free of domination.

As we have seen, however, the economic model itself lacks universal applicability. At the level of national politics especially, where the economic model's policy framework of resourced exit and enhanced competition must be created and maintained, there is simply no substitute for voice, for the tricky business of political entrepreneurship and coalition building in a democratic system. Moreover, given the high cost of international migration, inter alia, the economic model is unlikely to have much relevance to the national state, and at lower levels of the state exit costs will usually remain high enough to require a substantial role for the political model. Even in the domestic and economic spheres the political model will have to play an auxiliary role at times: as I noted in the conclusions to Chapters 2 and 3, when agency is compromised by psychological or physical abuse, immaturity, senility, mental disability, or legal disempowerment, state regulatory interventions will often be justified. In short, neither the economic nor the political model can be treated as a one-size-fits-all solution to every problem of domination in every sphere of human existence.

What general lessons can we draw, then, regarding the applicability of these models? As I discussed in Chapter 4, our job is to find optimal mixes of accountability mechanisms, mixes that are sure to vary across social contexts. On the basis of the arguments made so far in this book, I would suggest the following rule of thumb for the task of institutional design: in any given social context—whether domestic, economic, or political—the economic model is more promising as a supplement to or even a substitute for the political model, *ceteris paribus*, the more it is the case that these three enabling conditions hold:

1. full psychological agency of market participants, including all the relevant technical and prudential capacities for active and effective involvement in the marketplace;
2. full legal agency of market participants, including secure legal status, equality before the law, and protection of a set of basic freedoms and opportunities (such as rights to move, associate, contract, and own property); and
3. exit costs that either are already low or can realistically be made so through state action.

Because these conditions are met to different degrees in different areas of human life, the relative strength of the economic model varies both within and between spheres. Again, like the political model, it is far from being a panacea.

In the central chapters of this book, however, we have seen the many surprising ways that exit-oriented state interventionism can limit domination, at times in conjunction with the political model but frequently alone. For fully competent adults with legal status, the economic model can usually serve as an effective guarantee of republican freedom in the spheres of family and market without the assistance of the political model. Even in the sphere of the state, the economic model can provide a powerful supplement to the political model, working in tandem with it to diminish domination at the provincial and especially the local level. Also, there are reasons to believe that the economic model will become increasingly relevant across all spheres over time. For example, changes in the structure of economic activity—such as the transition from an industrial economy to a service economy, with its need for more educated workers prompting greater investment in human capital—may enhance psychological agency, thereby enabling a greater role to be played by the economic model.

None of this is meant to suggest that we should treat the economic model as even a strong default, much less as a universal strategy for confronting domination. Nonetheless, given the fact that neo-republicans have a long track record of overreliance on the political model, it might be a useful discipline for them to consider the economic model first when they deliberate about policy responses to domination, as a (temporary) corrective to certain mental habits and biases. Treating the economic model in this manner as a weak default will require neo-republicans to reorient their thinking about domination, obliging them to trade their social-democratic partialities for market-friendlier ones and to take the danger of state domination more seriously. By supporting policies like the basic income, they have already begun this transition, and I hope this book will persuade them to complete it.

I have repeatedly emphasized that the economic model is impossible to apply at the level of the national state. Might it become possible at some point in the future, though, and if so, what would this imply about the content of a global republicanism? Neo-republicans have only recently started to explore the implications of republicanism for global justice and international relations more widely.[1] I would therefore like to end the book with a preparatory sketch for an application of commercial republicanism to the international realm.

The cost of international migration is the main obstacle to its application, but in time the spread of open societies, economic growth, improved education, and reductions in transportation costs and language barriers (thanks in part to the adoption of English as the international lingua franca) could help us overcome it, at least sufficiently so to make the economic model a feasible competitor to the political model internationally. We should immediately acknowledge, however, that if republicans are likely to disagree with each other about exit-oriented state interventionism *within* the nation-state, they are even more likely to disagree about it in the international domain. Those favorable to such interventionism would no doubt point out that a variety of international economic and political

---

[1] See, for example, Buckinx et al. (2015) and Pettit (2010; 2014, especially ch. 6). I will reference the second of these Pettit works throughout my preparatory sketch.

institutions—including the International Monetary Fund, the World Bank, the United Nations, the European Union, and so forth—already exist and provide a rudimentary framework for peaceful interstate cooperation that could be expanded and deepened over time to encourage global political and economic competition and the resourced exit of citizens and firms across national boundaries. Just as Tiebout-model competition between local governments can, if enabled by fiscal federalism and enhanced mobility, limit the ability of local officials to exploit and dominate their residents, so its equivalent in the global arena might do the same to national officials, curbing abuses as extreme as totalitarianism or as mild as complicity with rent-seeking pressure groups. Those skeptical of such interventionism, though, would probably worry that any global political institutions powerful enough to realize this vision would themselves pose a threat to the world's population, creating a risk of state domination on an unprecedented scale.

Interestingly, these opposed republican ideas regarding international institutions can both be found in the political thought of a single republican, Immanuel Kant, and the way he resolved his own ambivalence about such institutions is instructive. In his political works, Kant fixated on the great evil of interstate war, in which rulers routinely exercise arbitrary power not merely over foreign peoples but over their own subjects as well. His solution to this problem relies heavily on an analogy: just as individuals can only hope to achieve domestic peace by jointly submitting to a civil constitution, so nations can only hope to attain international peace by mutually submitting to a cosmopolitan constitution, thus joining a state of nations *(Völkerstaat)* with coercive powers that each nation would have to obey for the sake of perpetual peace (1996, 307, 309, 328 [8:310–1, 312–13, 357]). A strong version of international republicanism thereby becomes the remedy to the residual ills of a merely national republicanism.

As attracted as Kant is to this remedy on theoretical grounds, however, he worries about its consequences in practice, and his unease with it—although present from the beginning—only grows with time. Even in his earliest discussion of a *Völkerstaat*, he notes that "if this condition of universal peace is still more dangerous to freedom ... by leading to the most fearful despotism (as has indeed happened more than once with states that have grown too large)," then alternative political means must be used (1996, 307–8 [8:311]). He elaborates upon this concern in "Toward Perpetual Peace," where he notes that an international state of nature would still be preferable to a "universal monarchy" or world republic, which would grow into a "soulless despotism" and, in the course of gobbling up smaller nations and extending its rule everywhere, would see its laws gradually weaken and anarchy return, leaving nothing but a "graveyard of freedom" in its wake (1996, 336 [8:367]). By the time he pens *The Metaphysics of Morals*, he realizes that these flaws are fatal to the idea of a *Völkerstaat* and even to perpetual peace itself, which he now refers to as an "unachievable idea" (1996, 487 [6:350]). The cure, in short, is worse than the disease, and the strong version of international republicanism must therefore be abandoned with regret.[2]

But all is not lost. The idea of perpetual peace, even if it is ultimately not achievable, may still be approachable through a league of nations *(Völkerbund)*, a free federalism "in accordance with a commonly agreed upon right of nations" that seeks peace but "does not look to acquiring any power of a state" (1996, 308, 327 [8:311, 356]). Its lack of coercive powers, however, limits its usefulness, so it must be supplemented by other means both political and economic. First, the participating nations must carry out internal political reform, making their civil constitutions ever more consistent with the "idea of the original contract," viz., that the "citizens of a state...must therefore give their free assent, through their representatives, not only to the waging of war in general but also to each particular declaration of war" (1996, 308, 484 [8:311, 6:345–6]). Such a reform, by resting the fundamental war power in the hands of those least likely to exercise it, will make nations less bellicose and promote international peace: unlike their rulers, the people "will be very hesitant to begin such a bad game, since they would have to...take upon themselves all the hardships of war (such as...doing the fighting and paying the costs...)" (1996, 323 [8:350]). Second, the participating nations must recognize "cosmopolitan right," viz., a "right to hospitality [that] does not extend beyond the conditions which make it possible to *seek commerce*" (1996, 329 [8:358]). Kant argues that "the spirit of commerce... cannot coexist with war and...sooner or later takes hold of every nation"; once nations acquiesce to the "power of money," they will seek trade and peace out of "mutual self-interest," and warlike passions will gradually be displaced by businesslike interests (1996, 336–7 [8:368]; cf. Hirschman 1977).

These three elements of Kant's political program—a league of nations (external political republicanism), popular power (internal political republicanism), and *doux commerce* (economic republicanism)—constitute what we might call a *minimal global republicanism*, one focused on enabling law-governed human

---

[2] Pettit argues along similar lines: "in the abstract, a world state might work very well. But in a world where cultures vary enormously, agreed policymaking norms would be unlikely to crystallize in the way they can in a more closely connected society. And in a world where trust is often in short supply across cultural divides, there would be less likelihood of establishing those important unelected authorities...who could credibly claim to make decisions in line with shared standards....Thus the cause of democracy, articulated in terms of freedom, argues for a world of many states" (2014, 158; cf. Bohman 2007, 60).

relationships within and across borders without resort to a world state. I believe that a similar kind of minimal global republicanism could serve as the basis for an overlapping consensus between those republicans who are supportive of a global version of exit-oriented state interventionism and those who are more skeptical (Rawls 1993, 133–72). This form of global republicanism would support the free movement of goods, services, people, and ideas across national borders as well as the international norms, rules, and institutions that would make such movement possible, all without committing itself in advance to a *Völkerstaat*. Advocates of a more ambitious, global version of state interventionism could view this as merely a transitional form of international governance, one that is worthy of support in its own right but also one that they would hope to see expanded and deepened with the passage of time, so that exit rights from the nation-state could be made substantive, not merely formal, via resourcing and the promotion of international political and economic competition by a world state or federation with coercive power. Their support for minimal global republicanism would still be sincere instead of strategic, however, because they would only sanction a transition to such coercive international institutions on the condition that long experience with the voluntaristic form had reduced fears of a "soulless despotism" and boosted confidence that global governance could be truly republican. Skeptics of this more ambitious global agenda, however, could view such a minimal global republicanism as approximating the final form of international governance, confident that lengthy experience will heighten rather than reduce fears of domination by a world state and thus buttress the status quo.

What would such a minimal global republicanism look like and require? It should involve a set of commitments that republicans of all stripes can ratify and would therefore need to focus narrowly on free trade, free migration, and the norms, rules, and institutions required to facilitate them. As for free trade, we have long experience with various rounds of the General Agreement on Tariffs and Trade, regional trade agreements (e.g., the North American Free Trade Agreement and the Treaty of Rome), and their varied international enforcement mechanisms (e.g., the World Trade Organization, the European Union, etc.), and this experience will prove invaluable in our ongoing efforts to further reduce tariffs—already at historically low levels—as well as non-tariff barriers such as quotas, discriminatory health-and-safety standards, etc. Unrestrained free trade at the global level would provide enormous benefits to consumers now exploited and dominated by their so-called "national champions" (i.e., national monopolists and oligopolists), who frequently use demagogic means to keep their industries insulated from foreign competition. It would also constitute a victory for developing countries who have long fought for market access in wealthier ones: as Pettit points out, the

Cairns Group of agricultural producers has often confronted the United States, European Union, and Japan in GATT/WTO negotiations over trade liberalization, whether by securing the Agreement on Agriculture in the Uruguay Round or blocking the efforts of wealthy nations to protect their own farmers in the Doha Round, but much work remains to be done before global free trade is fully realized (2014, 173; cf. Laborde and Ronzoni 2015).

Nowhere, however, is the demagoguery more ubiquitous and more morally repulsive than in debates on immigration. Free migration would again provide substantial economic benefits by not only reducing the effectiveness of national and regional labor cartels but also giving workers another way to escape local labor monopsonies and oligopsonies that are distressingly common in developing countries, where poor transportation networks, ineffective antitrust authorities, and limited or nonexistent welfare systems lock workers into abusive employment relations. Despite some progress over time (e.g., the free movement of labor within the European Union), advanced industrial nations—including immigrant societies such as the USA, Canada, and Australia—have continued to pursue exclusionary immigration policies, and the debate over immigration in both North America and Europe has become increasingly toxic over the past decade. Progress on this essential element of a minimal global republicanism has stalled and probably gone into reverse, and until labor is given the same rights of free international movement that capital largely enjoys, republicanism's goal of non-domination in labor markets will never be fully realized.

These economic benefits of free migration, important as they are, pale beside the benefits it can offer to refugees from totalitarian and authoritarian regimes worldwide, which remain the greatest menace to republican liberty internationally. The one-party states of North Korea, Cuba, and China and the pseudo-democracies of Iran, Russia, and Venezuela exercise arbitrary power over their own citizens on an ongoing basis through corruption, censorship, illegal detention, and the imprisonment, torture, and execution of political dissidents. Though we are morally obligated to use political criticism and economic pressure to encourage the internal political changes that in time will transform these nations into open societies and members in good standing of the global order, the most important action we can immediately take is to open our borders to the victims of these regimes. As I argued in Chapter 4, voice and exit worked in tandem to undermine the East-German dictatorship, with exit not only draining the state of workers (and potential hostages) but also amplifying the voices of those who remained behind; escaping from a dysfunctional system can put additional pressure on that system and encourage reform, especially if it sets an example for others and heightens public consciousness of the system's failure.

Even if these changes were never to occur, however, we would still advance freedom as non-domination by simply admitting these refugees, who as a result would no longer have to suffer under the abuses and degradations of arbitrary political authority.[3]

This relatively limited plan for a global political and economic order—what Kant would call a "republicanism of all states, together and separately" (1996, 491 [6:354])—would serve as a worthy object for our collective political energies. Ever mindful of Kant's warning that a world state would be a "soulless despotism" and a "graveyard of freedom," we would instead focus on the less ambitious but also safer project of promoting global competition and the free movement of products, people, and ideas across borders, whose success would be a humble but worthwhile approximation of Kant's own inspiring republican vision. Future generations, more experienced in global governance than we can ever hope to be, might ultimately build the kind of world state that seemed too risky to our generation, but they could only do so on foundations previously laid by a more modest global republicanism.

---

[3] Pettit defines "oppressive" regimes as those that "offend against those [justiciable] human rights of its subjects," and he reviews "many modes of response [to them], ranging from condemnation to ostracism, economic sanction to military intervention" (2014, 179–81, 225n88). He fails to mention refugee policies in this particular context, though they avoid many of the political costs—both domestic and international—of economic and military interventions.

References

Adelman, Jeremy. 2013. *Worldly Philosopher: The Odyssey of Albert O. Hirschman.* Princeton: Princeton University Press.

Ali, Mukhtar, H. Cecil, and James Knoblett. 2001. "The Effects of Tax Rates and Enforcement Policies on Taxpayer Compliance: A Study of Self-Employed Taxpayers." *Atlantic Economic Journal* 29(2): 186–202.

Allen, Douglas, and Maggie Gallagher. 2007. "Does Divorce Law Affect the Divorce Rate?" *iMAPP Research Brief* 1(1): 1–29.

Amato, Paul. 2010. "Research on Divorce: Continuing Trends and New Developments." *Journal of Marriage and Family* 72(3): 650–66.

Amis, Kingsley. 2013. *The Alteration.* New York: New York Review Books Classics.

Andreoni, James. 1993. "An Experimental Test of the Public-Goods Crowding-Out Hypothesis." *American Economic Review* 83(5): 1317–27.

Appelbaum, Binyamin. 2015. "Voucher Expansion Would Encourage More Low-Income Families to Move Out." *New York Times* (July 7).

Auty, Richard. 1993. *Sustaining Development in Mineral Economies: The Resource Curse Thesis.* London and New York: Routledge.

Baker, Elizabeth, Laura Sanchez, Steven Nock, and James Wright. 2009. "Covenant Marriage and the Sanctification of Gendered Marital Roles." *Journal of Family Issues* 30(2): 147–78.

Barry, Brian. 1974. "Review Article: *Exit, Voice, and Loyalty.*" *British Journal of Political Science* 4(1): 79–107.

Baumol, William, John Panzar, and Robert Willig. 1982. *Contestable Markets and the Theory of Industry Structure.* San Diego: Harcourt Brace Jovanovich.

Becker, Gary. 1973. "A Theory of Marriage: Part I." *Journal of Political Economy* 81(4): 813–46.

Becker, Gary. 1993. *A Treatise on the Family.* Cambridge, MA: Harvard University Press.

Besson, Samantha, and José Luis Martí, eds. 2009. *Legal Republicanism: National and International Perspectives.* Oxford: Oxford University Press.

Bhaskar, V., Alan Manning, and Ted To. 2002. "Oligopsony and Monopsonistic Competition in Labor Markets." *Journal of Economic Perspectives* 16(2): 155–74.

Bohman, James. 2007. *Democracy across Borders: From Demos to Demoi.* Cambridge, MA: MIT Press.

Bohman, James. 2009. "Cosmopolitan Republicanism and the Rule of Law." In Besson and Martí, *Legal Republicanism*, pp. 60–77.

Bohman, James. 2011. "Children and the Rights of Citizens: Nondomination and Intergenerational Justice." *The ANNALS of the American Academy of Political and Social Science* 633(1): 128–40.

Brennan, Jason, and Peter Jaworski. 2015. "Markets without Symbolic Limits." *Ethics* 125(4): 1053–77.

Brown, John. 1995. *The British Welfare State: A Critical History.* Oxford: Blackwell.
Buchanan, James. 1996. "Federalism and Individual Sovereignty." *Cato Journal* 15(2/3): 259–68.
Buchanan, James, and Gordon Tullock. 1962. *The Calculus of Consent: Logical Foundations of Constitutional Democracy.* Ann Arbor: University of Michigan Press.
Buckinx, Barbara, Jonathan Trejo-Mathys, and Timothy Waligore, eds. 2015. *Domination and Global Political Justice: Conceptual, Historical, and Institutional Perspectives.* New York: Routledge.
Bureau of Labor Statistics. 2014. *American Time Use Survey—2013 Results.* http://www.bls.gov/news.release/pdf/atus.pdf
Bureau of Labor Statistics. 2015. *Economic News Release: Union Members Survey (2014).* http://www.bls.gov/news.release/union2.nr0.htm
Card, David, and Alan Krueger. 1997. *Myth and Measurement: The New Economics of the Minimum Wage.* Princeton, NJ: Princeton University Press.
Catalano, Shannan. 2013. *Intimate Partner Violence: Attributes of Victimization, 1993–2011.* Washington, DC: Bureau of Justice Statistics (US Department of Justice).
Cebula, Richard. 2004. "Income Tax Evasion Revisited: The Impact of Interest-Rate Yields on Tax-Free Municipal Bonds." *Southern Economic Journal* 71(2): 418–23.
Central Intelligence Agency. 2014. *The World Factbook.* https://www.cia.gov/library/publications/the-world-factbook/rankorder/2127rank.html
Chetty, Raj, and Nathaniel Hendren. 2015. "The Impacts of Neighborhoods on Intergenerational Mobility: Childhood Exposure Effects and County-Level Estimates." http://www.equality-of-opportunity.org/images/nbhds_paper.pdf
Chetty, Raj, Nathaniel Hendren, and Lawrence Katz. 2015. "The Effects of Exposure to Better Neighborhoods on Children: New Evidence from the Moving to Opportunity Experiment." http://www.equality-of-opportunity.org/images/mto_paper.pdf
Chetty, Raj, Nathaniel Hendren, Patrick Kline, and Emmanuel Saez. 2014. "Where is the Land of Opportunity? The Geography of Intergenerational Mobility in the United States." National Bureau of Economic Research. Working Paper No. 19843.
Cho, Hyunkag, and Dina Wilke. 2005. "How Has the Violence Against Women Act Affected the Response of the Criminal Justice System to Domestic Violence?" *Journal of Sociology and Social Welfare* 33(4): 125–39.
Clark, Gregory. 2007. *A Farewell to Alms: A Brief Economic History of the World.* Princeton: Princeton University Press.
Clark, Stephen. 2003. "Progressive Federalism? A Gay Liberationist Perspective." *Albany Law Review* 66(3): 719–57.
Clotfelter, Charles. 1983. "Tax Evasion and Tax Rates: An Analysis of Individual Returns." *Review of Economics and Statistics* 65(3): 363–73.
Congressional Budget Office. 2014. "The Federal Budget in 2013." https://www.cbo.gov/sites/default/files/45278-Budget_Overall_Final.pdf
Corfield v. Coryell, 6 Fed. Cas. 546 (1823).
Costa, Victoria. 2013. "Is Neo-Republicanism Bad for Women?" *Hypatia* 28(4): 921–36.
CREDO (Center for Research on Education Outcomes). 2013. *National Charter School Study.* Palo Alto, CA: CREDO at Stanford University.

Dagger, Richard. 1997. *Civic Virtues: Rights, Citizenship, and Republican Liberalism.* Oxford: Oxford University Press.

Dagger, Richard. 2006. "Neo-republicanism and the Civic Economy." *Politics, Philosophy, and Economics* 5(2): 151–73.

Daniel, Cletus. 1981. *Bitter Harvest: A History of California Farmworkers, 1870–1941.* Ithaca: Cornell University Press.

Debreu, Gerard. 1959. *Theory of Value: An Axiomatic Analysis of Economic Equilibrium.* New Haven: Yale University Press.

Demick, Barbara. 2010. *Nothing to Envy: Ordinary Lives in North Korea.* New York: Spiegel & Grau.

Dewan, Shaila. 2014. "Law Lets I.R.S. Seize Accounts on Suspicion, No Crime Required." *New York Times* (October 25).

de Dijn, Annelien. 2014. "Was Montesquieu a Liberal Republican?" *Review of Politics* 76(1): 21–41.

Dompe, Stewart, and Adam Smith. 2014. "Regulation of Platform Markets in Transportation." *Mercatus on Policy* (October 27). http://mercatus.org/sites/default/files/Dompe-Smith-Platform-Markets-MOP.pdf.

Douglass, Robin. 2012. "Montesquieu and Modern Republicanism." *Political Studies* 60(3): 703–19.

Downs, Anthony. 1957. *An Economic Theory of Democracy.* New York: Harper and Row.

The Economist. 2013. "Pennies from Heaven" (October 26). http://www.economist.com/news/international/215883850giving-money-directly-poor-people-works-surprisingly-well-it-cannot-deal

The Economist. 2015. "Europe v Google: Nothing to Stand On" (April 18). http://www.economist.com/news/business-and-finance/21648606-google

The Economist. 2016. "Terms of enlargement: Clever reforms can reduce the power of NIMBYs and cut housing costs" (April 16). http://www.economist.com/node/21696949

Eisenberg, Avigail, and Jeff Spinner-Halev, eds. 2005. *Minorities within Minorities: Equality, Rights and Diversity.* Cambridge: Cambridge University Press.

Elias, Norbert. 1983. *The Court Society,* trans. Edmund Jephcott. Oxford: Basil Blackwell.

Elster, Jon. 1986. "The Market and the Forum: Three Varieties of Political Theory." In Jon Elster and Aanund Hylland, eds., *Foundations of Social Choice Theory.* Cambridge: Cambridge University Press, pp. 103–32.

Epple, Dennis, and Allan Zelenitz. 1981. "The Implications of Competition among Jurisdictions: Does Tiebout Need Politics?" *Journal of Political Economy* 89(6): 1197–217.

Epstein, Richard. 1992. "Exit Rights Under Federalism." *Law and Contemporary Problems* 55(1): 147–65.

European Union. 1957. *Treaty Establishing the European Community (Consolidated Version), Rome Treaty.* http://www.refworld.org/docid/3ae6b39c0.html

Feige, Edgar. 1994. "The Underground Economy and the Currency Enigma." *Public Finance* 49 (Supplement): 119–36.

Ferejohn, John. 2001. "Pettit's Republic." *The Monist* 84(1): 77–97.

Filmer, Robert. 1991. *Patriarcha and Other Writings*, ed. Johann Sommerville. Cambridge: Cambridge University Press.

Fischel, William. 2001. *The Homevoter Hypothesis: How Home Values Influence Local Government Taxation, School Finance, and Land-Use Policies*. Cambridge, MA: Harvard University Press.

Fischel, William, ed. 2006. *The Tiebout Model at Fifty: Essays in Public Economics in Honor of Wallace Oates*. Cambridge, MA: Lincoln Institute of Land Policy.

Foucault, Michel. 2008. *The Birth of Biopolitics: Lectures at the Collège de France, 1978–79*, ed. Michel Senellart, trans. Graham Burchell. New York: Palgrave Macmillan.

Friedman, Milton. 1962. *Capitalism and Freedom*. Chicago: University of Chicago Press.

Frier, Bruce, and Thomas McGinn. 2004. *A Casebook on Roman Family Law*. Oxford: Oxford University Press.

Gaus, Gerald. 2003. "Backwards into the Future: Neo-republicanism as a Postsocialist Critique of Market Society." *Social Philosophy and Policy* 20(1): 59–91.

Gleason, Philip, Melissa Clark, Christina Clark Tuttle, and Emily Dwoyer. 2010. *The Evaluation of Charter School Impacts: Executive Summary*. Washington, DC: US Department of Education, Institute of Education Sciences, National Center for Education Evaluation and Regional Assistance. http://ies.ed.gov/ncee/pubs/20104029/pdf/20104030.pdf

Goldin, Claudia. 2006. "The Quiet Revolution That Transformed Women's Employment, Education, and Family." *American Economic Review* 96(2): 1–21.

Goldin, Claudia. 2014. "A Grand Gender Convergence: Its Last Chapter." *American Economic Review* 104(4): 1091–119.

Gourevitch, Alex. 2013. "Labor Republicanism and the Transformation of Work." *Political Theory* 41(4): 591–617.

Gourevitch, Alex. 2014. *From Slavery to the Cooperative Commonwealth: Labor and Republican Liberty in the Nineteenth Century*. New York: Cambridge University Press.

Grossbard-Shechtman, Shoshana. 1995. "Marriage Market Models." In Mariano Tommasi and Kathryn Ierulli, eds., *The New Economics of Human Behavior*. Cambridge: Cambridge University Press, pp. 92–112.

Halbrook, Stephen. 1984. *That Every Man Be Armed: The Evolution of a Constitutional Right*. Albuquerque: University of New Mexico Press.

Hamburger, Philip. 2014. *Is Administrative Law Unlawful?* Chicago: University of Chicago Press.

Hanley, Ryan. 2008. "Commerce and Corruption: Rousseau's Diagnosis and Adam Smith's Cure." *European Journal of Political Theory* 7(2): 137–58.

Haskins, Ron. 2012. "Testimony before Budget Committee of U.S. House of Representatives" (April 17). http://www.brookings.edu/~/media/research/files/testimony/2012/4/17-means-testing-haskins/0417_means_testing_haskins

Hayek, Friedrich. 1948. *Individualism and Economic Order*. Chicago: University of Chicago Press.

Hayek, Friedrich. 1960. *The Constitution of Liberty*. Chicago: University of Chicago Press.

Hayek, Friedrich. 1982. *Law, Legislation, and Liberty: A New Statement of the Liberal Principles of Justice and Political Economy*. London: Routledge (3 Vols. in 1).

Health and Human Services. 2015. "2015 Poverty Guidelines." http://aspe.hhs.gov/poverty/15poverty.cfm#thresholds

Henderson, Vernon. 1985. "The Tiebout Model: Bring Back the Entrepreneurs." *Journal of Political Economy* 93(2): 248–64.

Herzog, Lisa. 2016. "The Normative Stakes of Economic Growth; Or, Why Adam Smith Does Not Rely on 'Trickle Down.'" *Journal of Politics* 78(1): 50–62.

Higgs, Robert. 1987. *Crisis and Leviathan: Critical Episodes in the Growth of American Government.* New York: Oxford University Press.

Hirschman, Albert. 1958. *The Strategy of Economic Development.* New Haven: Yale University Press.

Hirschman, Albert. 1970. *Exit, Voice, and Loyalty: Responses to Decline in Firms, Organizations, and States.* Cambridge, MA: Harvard University Press.

Hirschman, Albert. 1977. *The Passions and the Interests: Political Arguments for Capitalism before Its Triumph.* Princeton: Princeton University Press.

Hirschman, Albert. 1991. *The Rhetoric of Reaction: Perversity, Futility, Jeopardy.* Cambridge, MA: Belknap Press.

Hoxby, Caroline. 2000. "Does Competition among Public Schools Benefit Students and Taxpayers?" *American Economic Review* 90(5): 1209–38.

Hsieh, Nien-hê. 2005. "Rawlsian Justice and Workplace Republicanism." *Social Theory and Practice* 31(1): 115–42.

Hunter-Gault, Charlayne. 2014. "Hard Times at Howard U." *New York Times* (February 4).

Huntington, Samuel. 1952. "The Marasmus of the ICC: The Commission, the Railroads, and the Public Interest." *Yale Law Journal* 61(4): 467–509.

Huntington, Samuel. 1993. *The Third Wave: Democratization in the Late Twentieth Century.* Norman, OK: University of Oklahoma Press.

Ihrke, David. 2014. *Reason for Moving: 2012 to 2013 (Population Characteristics).* Washington, DC: US Census Bureau.

Inman, Robert. 2006. "Commentary [on Oates 2006]." In Fischel, *The Tiebout Model at Fifty*, pp. 46–54.

Isen, Adam, and Betsey Stevenson. 2010. "Women's Education and Family Behavior: Trends in Marriage, Divorce, and Fertility." In John Shoven, ed., *Demography and the Economy.* Chicago: University of Chicago Press, pp. 107–42.

Jansen, Jim. 2010. "Use of the Internet in Higher-Income Households." Pew Research Center's Internet & American Life Project. http://www.pewinternet.org/files/old-media//Files/Reports/2010/PIP-Better-off-households-final.pdf

Kant, Immanuel. 1996. *Practical Philosophy*, trans. and ed. Mary Gregor. Cambridge: Cambridge University Press.

Kaplan, Greg, and Sam Schulhofer-Wohl. 2013. "Understanding the Long-Run Decline in Interstate Migration." Federal Reserve Bank of Minneapolis. Working Paper 697.

Kleiner, Morris. 2013. *Stages of Occupational Regulation: Analysis of Case Studies.* Kalamazoo: W.E. Upjohn Institute for Employment Research.

Kleiner, Morris, and Alan Krueger. 2013. "Analyzing the Extent and Influence of Occupational Licensing on the Labor Market." *Journal of Labor Economics* 31(2): S173–S202.

Klepper, Steven, Daniel Nagin, and Stephen Spurr. 1991. "Tax Rates, Tax Compliance, and the Reporting of Long-Term Capital Gains." *Public Finance* 46(2): 236–51.

Kling, Jeffrey, Jeffrey Liebman, and Lawrence Katz. 2007. "Experimental Analysis of Neighborhood Effects." *Econometrica* 75(1): 83–119.

Koss, Mary. 2000. "Blame, Shame, and Community: Justice Responses to Violence Against Women." *American Psychologist* 55(11): 1332–43.

Krause, Sharon. 2013. "Beyond Non-Domination: Agency, Inequality and the Meaning of Freedom." *Philosophy and Social Criticism* 39(2): 187–208.

Kukathas, Chandran. 2003. *The Liberal Archipelago: A Theory of Diversity and Freedom*. Oxford: Oxford University Press.

Kymlicka, Will. 2001. "Minority Nationalism and Multination Federalism." In *Politics in the Vernacular*. Oxford: Oxford University Press, pp. 91–119.

Laborde, Cécile. 2008. *Critical Republicanism: The Hijab Controversy and Political Philosophy*. Oxford: Oxford University Press.

Laborde, Cécile, and Miriam Ronzoni. 2015. "What is a Free State? Republican Internationalism and Globalisation." *Political Studies*. Forthcoming, Early View.

Laffont, Jean-Jacques, and Jean Tirole. 1991. "The Politics of Government Decision-Making: A Theory of Regulatory Capture." *Quarterly Journal of Economics* 106(4): 1089–127.

Levine, Michael, and Jennifer Forrence. 1990. "Regulatory Capture, Public Interest, and the Public Agenda: Toward a Synthesis." *Journal of Law, Economics, & Organization* 6 (Special Issue): 167–98.

Locke, John. 1988. *Two Treatises of Government*, ed. Peter Laslett. Cambridge: Cambridge University Press.

Lovett, Frank. 2009. "Domination and Distributive Justice." *Journal of Politics* 71(3): 817–30.

Lovett, Frank. 2010. *A General Theory of Domination and Justice*. Oxford: Oxford University Press.

Lovett, Frank, and Philip Pettit. 2009. "Neorepublicanism: A Normative and Institutional Research Program." *Annual Review of Political Science* 12: 11–29.

Lovett, Frank, and Gregory Whitfield. 2016. "Republicanism, Perfectionism, and Neutrality." *Journal of Political Philosophy* 24(1): 120–34.

Lowrey, Annie. 2014. "What's the Matter with Eastern Kentucky?" *New York Times Magazine* (June 26).

Lunsing, Wim. 2003. "'Parasite' and 'Non-parasite' Singles: Japanese Journalists and Scholars Taking Positions." *Social Science Japan Journal* 6(2): 261–5.

MacGilvray, Eric. 2011. *The Invention of Market Freedom*. New York: Cambridge University Press.

McCraw, Thomas. 1986. *Prophets of Regulation*. Cambridge, MA: Harvard University Press.

McMahon, Christopher. 2005. "The Indeterminacy of Republican Policy." *Philosophy and Public Affairs* 33(1): 67–93.

Mercier, Laurie. 2001. *Anaconda: Labor, Community, and Culture in Montana's Smelter City*. Urbana: University of Illinois Press.

Mill, John Stuart. 1991. *On Liberty and Other Essays*, ed. John Gray. Oxford: Oxford University Press.

Milton, John. 2010. *The Divorce Tracts of John Milton: Texts and Contexts*, eds. Sara van den Berg and W. Scott Howard. Pittsburgh: Duquesne University Press.

Montaigne, Michel de. 1993. *The Complete Essays*, ed. and trans. M. A. Screech. London: Penguin Classics.
Montesquieu, Charles de Secondat, baron de. 1989. *The Spirit of the Laws*, trans. and ed. Anne Cohler, Basia Miller, and Harold Stone. Cambridge: Cambridge University Press.
Moretti, Enrico. 2012. *The New Geography of Jobs*. Boston: Houghton Mifflin Harcourt.
Neumark, David, and William Wascher. 2008. *Minimum Wages*. Cambridge, MA: MIT Press.
Nicholson, Walter. 1995. *Microeconomic Theory*. Fort Worth: Dryden Press. Sixth Edition.
Noble, Charles. 1997. *Welfare as We Knew It: A Political History of the American Welfare State*. New York: Oxford University Press.
Nock, Steven, Laura Sanchez, and James Wright. 2008. *Covenant Marriage: The Movement to Reclaim Tradition in America*. New Brunswick, NJ: Rutgers University Press.
Norman, Wayne. 1994. "Towards a Philosophy of Federalism." In Judith Baker, ed., *Group Rights*. Toronto: University of Toronto Press, pp. 79–100.
Norman, Wayne. 2006. *Negotiating Nationalism: Nation-building, Federalism, and Secession in the Multinational State*. Oxford: Oxford University Press.
Nozick, Robert. 1974. *Anarchy, State, and Utopia*. New York: Basic Books.
Oates, Wallace. 1969. "The Effects of Property Taxes and Local Public Spending on Property Values: An Empirical Study of Tax Capitalization and the Tiebout Hypothesis." *Journal of Political Economy* 77(6): 957–71.
Oates, Wallace. 1972. *Fiscal Federalism*. New York: Harcourt Brace Jovanovich.
Oates, Wallace. 1999. "An Essay on Fiscal Federalism." *Journal of Economic Literature* 37(3): 1120–49.
Oates, Wallace. 2006. "The Many Faces of the Tiebout Model." In Fischel, *The Tiebout Model at Fifty*, pp. 21–45.
OED Online. 2015. Oxford University Press.
Okin, Susan. 1999. *Is Multiculturalism Bad for Women?* Eds. Joshua Cohen, Matthew Howard, and Martha Nussbaum. Princeton: Princeton University Press.
Olson, Mancur. 1971. *The Logic of Collective Action*. Cambridge, MA: Harvard University Press.
Pangle, Thomas. 1973. *Montesquieu's Philosophy of Liberalism: A Commentary on "The Spirit of the Laws."* Chicago: University of Chicago Press.
Pappas, Marcia. 2010. "No-Fault Divorce." National Organization for Women, New York State. http://www.nownys.org/leg_memos_2010/no_fault_divorce.pdf
Parfit, Derek. 1997. "Equality and Priority." *Ratio* 10(3): 202–21.
Pateman, Carole. 1988. *The Sexual Contract*. Palo Alto: Stanford University Press.
Peterman, Larry, and Tiffany Jones. 2003. "Defending Family Privacy." *Journal of Law and Family Studies* 5(1): 71–98.
Pettit, Philip. 1995. "The Virtual Reality of *Homo Economicus*." *The Monist* 78(3): 308–29.
Pettit, Philip. 1996. "Freedom as Antipower." *Ethics* 106(3): 576–604.
Pettit, Philip. 1997. *Republicanism: A Theory of Freedom and Government*. New York: Oxford University Press.
Pettit, Philip. 2001. *A Theory of Freedom: From the Psychology to the Politics of Agency*. Oxford: Oxford University Press.

Pettit, Philip. 2006a. "The Determinacy of Republican Policy: A Reply to McMahon." *Philosophy and Public Affairs* 34(3): 275–83.

Pettit, Philip. 2006b. "Freedom in the Market." *Politics, Philosophy, and Economics* 5(2): 131–49.

Pettit, Philip. 2007. "A Republican Right to Basic Income?" *Basic Income Studies* 2(2): 1–8.

Pettit, Philip. 2010. "A Republican Law of Peoples." *European Journal of Political Theory* 9(1): 70–94.

Pettit, Philip. 2012. *On the People's Terms: A Republican Theory and Model of Democracy*. Cambridge: Cambridge University Press.

Pettit, Philip. 2014. *Just Freedom: A Moral Compass for a Complex World*. New York: W. W. Norton and Company.

Pew Research Center. 2013. *Modern Parenthood: Roles of Moms and Dads Converge as They Balance Work and Family*. Washington, DC: Pew Research Center. http://www.pewsocialtrends.org/files/2013/03/FINAL_modern_parenthood_03-2013.pdf

Phillips, Anne. 2000. "Feminism and Republicanism: Is this a Plausible Alliance?" *Journal of Political Philosophy* 8(2): 279–93.

Phillips, Roderick. 1988. *Putting Asunder: A History of Divorce in Western Society*. Cambridge: Cambridge University Press.

Pierce v. Society of Sisters, 268 U.S. 510 (1925).

Plato. 1991. *The Republic of Plato*, ed. and trans. Allan Bloom. New York: Basic Books.

Publius (Alexander Hamilton, James Madison, and John Jay). 2003. *The Federalist*, ed. Terence Ball. Cambridge: Cambridge University Press.

Qian, Yingyi, and Gérard Roland. 1998. "Federalism and the Soft Budget Constraint." *American Economic Review* 88(5): 1143–62.

Rahe, Paul. 2009. *Montesquieu and the Logic of Liberty: War, Religion, Climate, Terrain, Technology, Uneasiness of Mind, the Spirit of Political Vigilance, and the Foundations of the Modern Republic*. New Haven: Yale University Press.

Rasmussen, Dennis. 2008. *The Problems and Promise of Commercial Society: Adam Smith's Response to Rousseau*. State College: Penn State University Press.

Rawls, John. 1993. *Political Liberalism*. New York: Columbia University Press.

Rawls, John. 2001. *Justice as Fairness: A Restatement*. Cambridge: Harvard University Press.

Roberts, Andrew. 2014. "A Republican Account of the Value of Privacy." *European Journal of Political Theory* 14(3): 1–25.

Roemer, John. 1996. *Egalitarian Perspectives: Essays in Philosophical Economics*. Cambridge: Cambridge University Press.

Rosenblum, Nancy. 1989. *Membership and Morals: The Personal Uses of Pluralism in America*. Princeton: Princeton University Press.

Rousseau, Jean-Jacques. 1997. *The Social Contract and Other Later Political Writings*, trans. and ed. Victor Gourevitch. Cambridge: Cambridge University Press.

Rousseau, Jean-Jacques. 2005. *The Plan for Perpetual Peace, On the Government of Poland, and Other Writings on History and Politics*, trans. and ed. Christopher Kelly. Hanover, NH: Dartmouth College Press.

Rousselière, Geneviève. 2016. "Rousseau on Freedom in Commercial Society." *American Journal of Political Science* 60(2): 352–63.

Saenz v. Roe, 526 U.S. 489 (1999).
Samuelson, Paul. 1954. "A Pure Theory of Public Expenditure." *The Review of Economics and Statistics* 36(4): 387–9.
Sandel, Michael. 1996. *Democracy's Discontent: America in Search of a Public Philosophy*. Cambridge, MA: Harvard University Press.
Sandel, Michael. 2012. *What Money Can't Buy: The Moral Limits of Markets*. New York: Farrar, Straus and Giroux.
Sapir, André. 2006. "Globalization and the Reform of European Social Models," *Journal of Common Market Studies* 44(2): 369–90.
Sarotte, Mary Elise. 2014. *The Collapse: The Accidental Opening of the Berlin Wall*. New York: Basic Books.
Schelling, Thomas. 1978. *Micromotives and Macrobehavior*. New York: Norton.
de Schutter, Helder. 2011. "Federalism as Fairness." *Journal of Political Philosophy* 19(2): 167–89.
Skinner, Quentin. 1998. *Liberty before Liberalism*. Cambridge: Cambridge University Press.
Smith, Adam. 1981. *An Inquiry Into the Nature and Causes of the Wealth of Nations*, eds. R. H. Campbell and A. S. Skinner. Indianapolis: Liberty Classics.
Somin, Ilya. 2010. "Foot Voting, Political Ignorance, and Constitutional Design." *Social Philosophy and Policy* 28(1): 202–27.
Sonstelie, Jon, and Paul Portney. 1978. "Profit-Maximizing Communities and the Theory of Local Public Expenditures." *Journal of Urban Economics* 5(2): 263–77.
Spitz, Jean-Fabien. 2009. "The '*défense républicaine*': Some Remarks about the Specificity of French Republicanism." In Besson and Martí, *Legal Republicanism*, pp. 281–97.
Stigler, George. 1975. *The Citizen and the State: Essays on Regulation*. Chicago: University of Chicago Press.
Streitfeld, David. 2014. "Silicon Valley Fights Order to Pay Bigger Settlement in Hiring Case." *New York Times* (September 5).
Sullivan, Daniel. 1989. "Monopsony Power in the Market for Nurses." *Journal of Law and Economics* 32(2), Part 2: S135–S178.
Tanzi, Vito, ed. 1982. *The Underground Economy in the United States and Abroad*. Lexington, MA: Lexington Books.
Taylor, Robert. 2013. "Market Freedom as Antipower." *American Political Science Review* 107(3): 593–602.
Taylor, Robert. 2014. "Illiberal Socialism." *Social Theory and Practice* 40(3): 433–60.
Thaler, Richard, and Cass Sunstein. 2009. *Nudge: Improving Decisions About Health, Wealth, and Happiness*. New York: Penguin Books.
Tiebout, Charles. 1956. "A Pure Theory of Local Expenditures." *Journal of Political Economy* 64(5): 416–24.
Tomasi, John. 2012. *Free Market Fairness*. Princeton: Princeton University Press.
US Census Bureau. 2013. *Current Population Survey*. Washington, DC: US Census Bureau. Geographic Mobility: 2012 to 2013. Table 28.
US Census Bureau. 2015. "State & County QuickFacts." http://quickfacts.census.gov/qfd/states/00000.html
van Parijs, Philippe. 2006. "Basic Income: A simple and powerful idea for the twenty-first century." In Erik Olin Wright, ed., *Redesigning Redistribution: Basic Income and*

Stakeholder Grants as Cornerstones for an Egalitarian Capitalism. New York: Verso, pp. 3–42.

Viscusi, Kip. 1983. *Risk by Choice: Regulating Health and Safety in the Workplace*. Cambridge, MA: Harvard University Press.

Walker, Lenore. 2006. "Battered Woman Syndrome: Empirical Findings." *Annals of the New York Academy of Sciences* 1087(1): 142–57.

Wallace, Jeremy. 2014. *Cities and Stability: Urbanization, Redistribution, and Regime Survival in China*. New York: Oxford University Press.

Walzer, Michael. 1983. *Spheres of Justice: A Defense of Pluralism and Equality*. New York: Basic Books.

Warren, Mark. 2011. "Voting with Your Feet: Exit-based Empowerment in Democratic Theory." *American Political Science Review* 105(4): 683–701.

Weingast, Barry. 1995. "The Economic Role of Political Institutions: Market-Preserving Federalism and Economic Development." *Journal of Law, Economics, & Organization* 11(1): 1–31.

Weinstock, Daniel. 2001. "Towards a Normative Theory of Federalism." *International Social Science Journal* 53(167): 75–83.

Weststeijn, Arthur. 2012. *Commercial Republicanism in the Dutch Golden Age: The Political Thought of Johan & Pieter de la Court*. Leiden: Brill.

White, Stuart. 2003. *The Civic Minimum: On the Rights and Obligations of Economic Citizenship*. Oxford: Oxford University Press.

Wilkerson, Isabel. 2010. *The Warmth of Other Suns: The Epic Story of America's Great Migration*. New York: Random House.

Wilson, William Julius. 1987. *The Truly Disadvantaged: The Inner City, the Underclass, and Public Policy*. Chicago: University of Chicago Press.

Wooders, Myrna. 1989. "A Tiebout Theorem." *Mathematical Social Sciences* 18(1): 33–55.

World Bank. 2014. *Labor Force Participation Rate, Female, By Country (2012 modeled ILO data)*. http://data.worldbank.org/indicator/SL.TLF.CACT.FE.ZS

Young, Iris Marion. 1989. "Polity and Group Difference: A Critique of the Ideal of Universal Citizenship." *Ethics* 99(2): 250–74.

Young, Iris Marion. 1990. *Justice and the Politics of Difference*. Princeton, NJ: Princeton University Press.

Young, Iris Marion. 2005. "Self-determination as Non-domination: Ideals applied to Palestine/Israel." *Ethnicities* 5(2): 139–59.

Index

Adelman, Jeremy 11
Affordable Care Act 77
African Americans, and mobility 74, 75
agriculture, and trade liberalization 114
Allen, Douglas and Maggie Gallagher 35, 42
Amato, Paul 35
Anaconda Copper Mining Company 49–50, 57
Anglo-Nordic market model 7, 49, 62n8, 63–4
antitrust action 8, 22, 48, 114
  and discretionary power 93, 94, 95
  and labor markets 24, 51, 53, 57, 65
arbitrary power 1, 108, 111
  and the charity market 94
  and exit 3–5, 18
  and interference 31, 58–9, 104
  and labor markets 22–3, 51–2, 60, 107
  and marital freedom 29, 32–3, 40
  and market competition 48, 54–7, 60
  and political freedom 66, 67, 69, 72, 78, 80–2, 84–5, 114–15
  and voice 2–3, 24
Auty, Richard 79

Baker, Elizabeth et al. 35
Barry, Brian 89–90
Becker, Gary 39
Berlin Wall 70
Bhaskar, V. et al. 51
Bohman, James 66
Brown, John 33
Bucer, Martin 41
Buchanan, James and Gordon Tullock 21

Cairns Group 114
Catalano, Shannan 28, 39
Chetty, Raj et al. 76, 78, 89
China, and mobility 70
Cho, Hyunkag and Dina Wilke 39, 44
Civil Aeronautics Board (CAB) 96
Clark, Stephen 74
class divisions, and exit 5, 13–14, 16–17, 76
  see also poverty
Constitution of Liberty, The (Hayek) 104
consumerism 102
  and mobility 5, 8, 71–2, 73–4, 87, 113
Corfield v. Coryell (1823) 75
covenant marriage 28–9, 35, 38, 40

Dagger, Richard 5, 8, 47–8, 54, 57, 61, 62, 68, 87–8, 89
Daniel, Cletus 65
Demick, Barbara 69
Democracy's Discontent (Sandel) 101
dental sector 52–3
discretionary power 6, 7, 8, 21
  and labor markets 50–1, 58–9
  and marital freedom 40–1
  and political power 73, 82, 84
  and state intervention 93–5, 97, 106
  and voice empowerment 22–4
divorce 6, 14, 28, 32, 33–4, 43
  and exit costs 15–16
  no-fault 35–8
  rates 34–5, 42
domination
  exit from 3–6, 85–8, 93
  and labor markets 50–4, 57–9, 99, 105
  and loyalty 89–90
  and marital freedom 28–36, 39–45
  and market power 46–9, 54, 60, 70–4
  and mobility 61–2, 70, 74–6, 91
  and political power 66–7, 80–1
  private 102–8
  and state intervention 8–9, 95–8, 100
  and voice empowerment 20–6, 57–60
  see also freedom as non-domination
Dompe, Stuart and Adam Smith 53
Downs, Anthony 85

Earned Income Tax Credit 93, 97
education
  effects of exit 13, 16–17
  and market power 60, 64
  and political power 73–4, 76, 105
  women's 33, 37
Eisenberg, Avigail and Jeff Spinner-Halev 37
electoral democracy 20–1
Elster, Jon 26
employment *see* labor market
Epple, Dennis and Allan Zelenitz 72
European Commission 93
Exit, Voice and Loyalty (Hirschman) 5–6, 11, 12, 89
exit costs 5, 8, 109
  and labor markets 52, 63
  and marital freedom 15–16, 28, 35–6, 38, 42–3
  and mobility 76–7, 108, 110

INDEX

family, and power 27
   exit for household dependents 44
   see also marriage
federalism 8*n*3, 19, 56, 63, 66–7, 89, 91, 95, 112
   fiscal 78–9, 82, 83, 85, 86, 88, 111
   and mobility 75, 77, 81, 85
Federalist Papers, The (Publius) 66
Ferejohn, John 44
Filmer, Robert 27
Fischel, William 72, 73, 80
freedom as non-domination 2, 4, 12*n*2, 30–1
   global solutions 111, 115
   Hayek's view of 104
   marital 27–40, 43–5
   and market power 46*n*1, 47–9, 51, 54, 56–62, 64
   political 67–70, 75, 78, 80–5, 90–1
   and state intervention 94, 101, 103–4, 109
free trade *see* trade liberalization
Friedman, Milton 11, 16, 53
Frier, Bruce and Thomas McGinn 27

Gaus, Gerald 47, 54
General Theory of Domination and Justice, A (Lovett) 2*n*1
German Democratic Republic 69–70, 90
global republicanism 9–10
   and mobility 110–11, 114–15
   trade liberalization 113–14
Goldin, Claudia 33, 36
Google 93
Gourevitch, Alex 62*n*8, 101, 106, 107
Great Migration 74
Grossbard-Shechtman, Shoshana 36

Halbrook, Stephen 86
Hamilton, Alexander 66
Haskins, Ron 89
Hayek, Friedrich A. 9, 92, 104–6
Higgs, Robert 96
Hirschman, Albert O. 25, 112
   definition of exit and voice 18
   dual exit thesis 5–6, 11–18, 34
   on loyalty 89
Honecker, Eric 69
Hoxby, Caroline 74
Hsieh, Nien-hê 4–5, 57–8

Ihrke, David 75
Inman, Robert 74, 79
Internet access 37, 76–7
Interstate Commerce Commission (ICC) 96
Isen, Adam and Betsey Stevenson 42

Jansen, Jim 76
Jordan, female labor force 33
jurisdictional competition 73–5, 78–80, 82–4, 88

Kant, Immanuel 10, 66
   and the "state of nations" 111–12, 115
Kaplan, Greg and Sam Schulhofer-Wohl 75
Kleiner, Morris 52, 53
Kling, Jeffrey et al. 77, 89
Koss, Mary 39
Krause, Sharon 107
Kukathas, Chandran 81*n*10
Kymlicka, Will 66

labor market
   exit from domination 29–30, 53–4, 57–9, 64–5, 99–100, 114
   gender discrimination 32–3, 34, 36
   and market power 49–54
   and mobility 53–4, 61, 76
   republican view 46–7, 101–2
   unions 52, 57, 60, 63–5, 105
   and voice empowerment 6–7, 22–4
licensing rules 52–3
Locke, John 86
Lovett, Frank 2*n*1, 4, 23, 29, 33, 37, 39, 54, 58, 68, 93, 94, 95*n*3, 100, 103
Lowrey, Annie 53

Madison, James 66
marital freedom 28–30, 34–8
   and domination 3, 27–8, 32–3
   and empowerment 39–42
market competition 12, 47–52, 108
   Anglo-Nordic model 49, 62*n*8, 63–4
   as antipower 38–9, 54–62
   global 113–15
   and marital freedom 29–30, 36–40, 43
   measures on 52–4, 93, 102–3, 106
   and political power 70–5, 79–80
Marx, Karl 51
McMahon, Christopher 48
Metaphysics of Morals, The (Kant) 112
migration *see* mobility
Mill, John Stuart 27, 29, 32, 33
Milton, John 6, 28–9, 34, 45
minimal global republicanism 9, 112–13
   and free migration 114–15
   and trade liberalization 113–14
minorities
   and marital freedom 36–7
   and mobility 72–3, 74, 75
mobility
   criticism of 87
   disadvantaged citizens 76–7, 88–9
   economic effects 80

and exit from domination 4, 5, 7-8, 9, 61, 74-6
global issues 110-11, 113-15
and political power 69-70
relocation vouchers 8, 53, 77-8, 89, 91
monopsony 24, 50-1
Montaigne, Michel de 43
Montesquieu, Charles de Secondat, baron de 66
Moretti, Enrico 54, 76, 77, 89
Move to Opportunity (MTO) 77, 89
multiculturalism
   and federalism 66-7
   and marital freedom 37

National Labor Relations Act 59-60
New Geography of Jobs, The (Moretti) 76
Nicholson, Walter 24, 50, 59
Noble, Charles 33
Nock, Steven 28, 35
no-fault divorce 6, 28, 33, 34-6, 38, 42
Norman, Wayne 66
North Korea 69, 114
Nozick, Robert 81n10, 103, 105

Oates, Wallace 71, 73, 78-9
Okin, Susan 37
Olson, Mancur 85
On the People's Terms: A Republican Theory and Model of Democracy (Pettit) 1, 3, 86

Pappas, Marcia 35, 36, 37
Pateman, Carole 33
Patriarcha and Other Writings (Filmer) 27
Peterman, Larry and Tiffany Jones 40
Pettit, Philip 2, 6, 24, 46n1, 93, 94, 95, 99, 100, 115n3
   on abuse of power 20-2
   on exit *vs.* voice 19
   on freedom as non-domination 1-4, 29-31, 38, 72n4, 103, 104, 106, 107, 112n2
   on global issues 113-14
   on marital freedom 34, 37
   on market power 47-8, 51-63
   on political power 66, 67, 68, 69, 73, 81-6
Phillips, Roderick 28, 29, 32, 33, 34, 37, 41
Plato 27
political freedom 68
   as antipower 81-4
   and citizens' voice 2-3
   and federalism 66-7
   and loyalty 89-90
   and market competition 70-2
   and mobility 69-70, 73-4, 85, 88-9
poverty
   and fiscal federalism 79
   and mobility 76-8, 88-9
   and welfare 93-4
private *vs.* public power 9, 97-100, 104-5, 108

"Pure Theory of Local Expenditures, A" (Tiebout) 70-1, 73

racial divisions 13-14, 74, 75
racial profiling 1, 72
Rawls, John 9, 36n5, 37, 61, 68, 98-9, 103, 113
refugees, and free migration 114-15
regulatory interventions 22-3, 44, 64, 109
   "blocked exchanges" 102-3
   and marriage 39-42
   regulatory capture 96, 106
religion, and marital exit 35, 38, 41, 42
relocation vouchers 8, 53, 77-8, 89, 91
Republic (Plato) 27
Republicanism: A Theory of Freedom and Government (Pettit) 1, 86
right-wing republicanism 91-2
   on exit-oriented policy 93-7
Roemer, John 26
Rosenblum, Nancy 102
Rousseau, Jean-Jacques 46-7, 66

Saenz v. Roe (1999) 17, 75
Samuelson, Paul 70-1
Sandel, Michael 9, 62, 101-4, 107
Sarotte, Mary Elise 69, 90
Schutter, Helder de 66
Skinner, Quentin 2n1
Smith, Adam 46-7, 53, 63, 64
Socialist Unity Party (GDR) 69
Social Security 96
Somin, Ilya 74
Spitz, Jean-Fabien 77
Stasi (Ministry for State Security, GDR) 69
state interventionism 2-3, 8-9, 96-8, 109-10
   criticism of 105-6
   direct and indirect empowerment 20-6
   in the domestic sphere 37-8, 39-40, 41-2
   in the economic sphere 6, 53-4, 58-9
   and political freedom 69-70
   welfare support 93-4
   see also political freedom
Stigler, George 96, 97
Strategy of Economic Development, The (Hirschman) 11
Streitfeld, David 53
Subjection of Women, The (Mill) 27, 29
subsidiarity 78
Sullivan, Daniel 51

taxes 4, 8, 9, 46, 71
   and discretionary power 73, 95, 97
   fiscal federalism 78-9, 82, 83, 85, 86, 88, 111
taxi companies, licensing 53
Thaler, Richard and Cass Sunstein 88-9
Tiebout, Charles 70-4, 79-80, 82n11, 84, 87, 111

Tomasi, John 92
"Toward Perpetual Peace" (Kant) 111
Trade Adjustment Assistance 53-4, 77
trade liberalization 9
   "blocked exchanges" 102-3
   global issues 113-14

unconditional basic income (UBI) 54, 94-5
unions, and voice empowerment 24, 57, 105
   market competition 52, 57, 60, 63-5, 106
United Farm Workers 65

Vestager, Margrethe 93
Violence Against Women Act (1994) 39, 44
Viscusi, Kip 53
voice empowerment 11-12
   definition 18
   direct and indirect 6-8, 20-5, 30, 39-40, 43-4, 65, 92
   and interference 2-3
   legal and illegal 19-20
   and political freedom 68-72, 80-1, 89-90
   risks of 58-60
   and the threat of exit 3-6, 13-18, 34-6, 57-8

Völkerstaat 111-12
voting 19-20, 85

wage discrimination 36, 50-2, 59, 100
Walker, Lenore 44
Wallace, Jeremy 70
Walzer, Michael 102
Warren, Mark 4n2, 19
Weinstock, Daniel 66
welfare support
   and discretionary power 93-4
   and fiscal federalism 78-9
   and marital power 33, 36, 41
   and market models 49, 55, 63
   and mobility 77
Wilkerson, Isabel 74
Wilson, William Julius 78
women
   and domination 3, 14, 27-9, 32-3
   marital exit 34-8
   and voice empowerment 39-43

Young, Iris Marion 66-7

Ingram Content Group UK Ltd.
Milton Keynes UK
UKHW021923180623
423657UK00003B/9